AN ORIENTAL LAND OF THE FREE

AN ORIENTAL LAND OF THE FREE

or

Life and Mission Work Among the Laos of Siam, Burma, China and Indo-China

By

JOHN HASKELL FREEMAN

GYAN

ISBN : 978-81-212-1527-5(HB)

First Published, 1910

Published, 2018

Published by

Gyan Publishing House
5, Ansari Road
Daryaganj, New Delhi-110002
Phone: 011-47034999, 9811692060
www.gyanbooks.com
E-mail: books@gyanbooks.com

Printed at: G. Print Process, Delhi.

AN ORIENTAL LAND OF THE FREE

CONTENTS

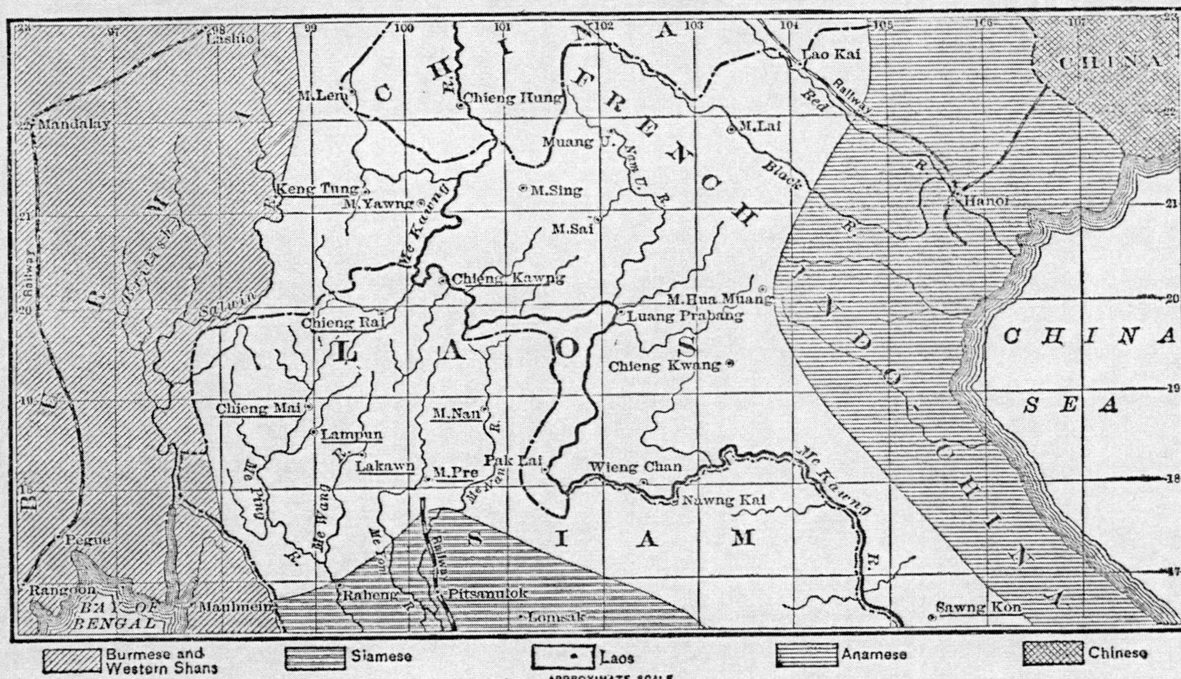

FIELD OF THE LAOS MISSION STATIONS UNDERLINED

EDITORIAL PREFACE

Mr. Freeman's furlough expired before he was able to see the manuscript of this book through the press. Dr. J. W. McKean, of Chieng Mai, has advised with the editor and has supplied the tables of distances between the Laos stations, and of the pronunciation of proper names. The only editorial changes worth mentioning have been a slight rearrangement of the original order of the chapters, the insertion of subsequent information received from Mr. Freeman, which will be found at the end of Chapter I, and the substitution of a set of questions on the text for the use of study classes.

T. H. P. SAILER.

March, 1910.

It is not the wish of the writer to forestall in any way that story. He rather seeks to answer for a larger audience a few of the questions that constantly have been asked of him as he told the story of the work of the kingdom in that far-away land. Who are the Laos? Where do they live? What is their religion? How do they make a living? What do they eat? What of their language, homes, schools? What special helps and hindrances does the missionary find in presenting the gospel to the Laos people? By picture, as well as by pen, he hopes to answer these questions regarding a people he has grown not only to respect but to love, for their physical prowess and mechanical skill; for their courtesy, kindness and openness of mind; for moral qualities that make them morally the peers of any race in Asia: our brothers for whom Christ died.

The writer hopes, above all, so to present the facts that the reader will be enabled to appreciate a people less known to the world than any that compares with them in numbers and in character, and to estimate fairly the responsibility that rests upon the Presbyterian Church in the United States of America for the evangelization of this great and growing people.

This little book is intended primarily for study classes and for reference, but it is hoped that the facts have been so presented as to commend it also to a larger public who are interested rather in strange people and lands than in mission work.

May this book interest some such readers in the greatest undertaking of the world of to-day.

The author wishes to express his obligation to James W. McKean, M. D., of Chieng Mai for material used in several chapters. Direct quotation has been acknowledged in each case, but several brief passages have been given in substance where quotation marks could not be used. Dr. McKean has also kindly consented to read proof, since the expiration of his furlough calls the writer back to his distant field.

For many illustrations, the writer is indebted to W. A. Briggs, M. D., of Chieng Rai, but he has been unable to ascertain the source of all the others. One is the work of Rev. W. F. Shields, another is probably the work of Mrs. Curtis, whose "The Laos of North Siam" has once been quoted and repeatedly referred to in these pages. Her book, which is published by the Presbyterian Board of Publication, gives the only connected account now available of life among the Laos. The only other book to which reference need be made is "A Thousand Miles on an Elephant in the Shan States" by Holt Hallett. Chapters in some books on Siam are devoted to the Laos people, but aside from these two books, only a few leaflets and the pages of the "Woman's Work" and of the "Assembly Herald," and "Missionary Review," especially for May, 1909, can be referred to as giving recent and full information regarding the Laos people or the work among them.

An Oriental Land of the Free

CHAPTER I

WHO ARE THE LAOS?

Siam and Laos have for many years been associated in the thoughts and gifts of the Presbyterian Church, but few even of those who read our mission publications, and contribute to work there carried on, understand clearly what and where "Laos" is. Fewer still have any real conception of the opportunity open to us as a church in that far-away land, or of the responsibility that rests upon us for the evangelization of a great and growing people. Laos is the name of a people, not of a political division. Poland once found its place on every map of Europe; to-day it cannot be found there, for the Poles are subjects of three powers, Russia, Prussia and Austria. So the Laos are subjects, not of Siam alone, but of France in Indo-China, of England, in the Shan States, of Burma, and of China in all her southern provinces.

The Tai Race in China

Two thousand years ago the Chinese occupied only the central part of what is now China. South of the Yangtse was the home of another race who called themselves Tai, or "The Free." About 250 B. C., the Chinese pushed southward across the

Yangtse and precipitated a conflict with the Tai race that continued for five hundred years; in a sense it still continues, for recent troubles in South China are at bottom a race conflict. Details of these wars fill many volumes of the Chinese annals.

The Tai Migration

We are concerned only with the result—the gradual movement of the Tai race southward and westward, till they reached the Bay of Bengal on the west and the Gulf of Siam on the south, and occupied the whole heart of the peninsula of Indo-China. Scattered aboriginal tribes, allied to the Tibetans, withdrew to the mountains, leaving to the Tai race the valleys and fertile plains that are still their home. These aborigines are now known as "the Hill Tribes" of Indo-China and Burma.

The Tai Left Behind in China

It must not be thought that the whole of the Tai race was driven out of China. A part was absorbed into the mass of the Chinese race, so that the Cantonese of to-day differ from the typical Chinese largely by an admixture of Tai blood and language. Non-Chinese people, many millions in all, are also found in all the southern provinces of China. Many—perhaps most—of these belong to the Tai race. Still the Tai migration was a great race movement, and its advance may well be compared to that of an army.

The Siamese

The left wing of this army of migration, moving southward parallel with the Chinese Sea, came in contact with the

Cambodians, who already possessed a civilization and a written language derived from India. Meeting and mingling with the Cambodians and Malays, later with the Chinese immigrants who came, (and are still coming) by sea, the left wing of the Tai army became the Siamese of to-day. Although mixed in blood and language, they still call themselves Tai. They occupy most of the southern half of the kingdom of Siam.

The Western Shans

The right wing, moving westward instead of south, that is, across the valleys of the Cambodia and Salween rivers, came in contact with the Burmese. Although their language was less modified than that of the Siamese, it is still quite distinct from typical Tai, and written in a different character. Their neighbors call them "Gnee-o," but English writers call all the race "Shans" and this branch of them "Western Shans." They give name to the so-called "Shan States" of Burma.

The Laos

The center or main body of the Tai migration came in contact with no other great race, and were profoundly modified by only one outside influence, that of the missionaries of Buddhism. They remain to-day practically unmixed in blood and unmixed in language, save for religious and polite terms derived from Pali, the sacred language of Buddhism. Although they call themselves Tai or "The Free," and are better entitled to that name than the Siamese and Western Shans, we prefer to use the name applied to them by the Siamese and French, and anglicized as Laos. Laos is really the name of one tribe and that not the largest, but it seems the most distinctive term to include those, and only those, whose vernacular and written character is the same as that in use in Chieng Mai, the largest city and, so to speak, the capital of the Laos.

The Extent of the Laos

Although they were formerly divided into tribes whose descendants retain some pecularities of dress and speech, and are found under the jurisdiction of four different governments,—Siam, Burma, China and French Indo-China—over an area as large as all France and Germany combined, they are one people. From southeast to northwest, following the general course of the Mekong or Cambodia River, one may travel a thousand miles in a straight line without reaching the limits of the Laos people. From the Salween on the west, almost to the China Sea on the east, throughout the northern half of Siam, on across the Shan States of Burma, and at least two hundred miles farther into the Yunnan province, China, the spoken language differs less than the English of Cornwall or Yorkshire differs from that of London.

The Hill Tribes

Isolated "hill tribes," each with its own language and customs, are found in many parts of this area, but they are islands in a sea; their only means of communication with each other and with the people of the plains is the Laos language, the *"lingua franca"* of them all. This, then, is the language through which this whole vast area must be won for Christ.

Population No reliable census of the Laos people in either of the four countries in which they are found has ever been made. Most so-called census enumerations aim to determine the number of adult males subject to poll tax; women and children are scarcely counted. The most reliable estimates give the Laos population of Siam as something over three million. French Indo-China and the Shan States of Burma are largely Laos, but more sparsely settled than Siam. Probably two millions is a conservative estimate of the Laos population in French and British territory. The people of the "Sip Song Punna" (Twelve States) in southern Yunnan are distinctly Laos, and northward and westward nearly to Tali-fu and Yunnan-fu, the language differs little, if at all, from typical Laos. Eastward and southward along the border of China and Tonquin are several million non-Chinese people, most of them probably Tai. We have little definite knowledge of them. These "Maotze" and other tribes like the Loi people of the island of Hainan, may differ somewhat widely from the Laos. Counting only the Tai people of Yunnan, not those farther east and south, the Laos in China may number two millions, and the total of all the Laos may be anywhere from six to ten millions.[1] At least ten times as numerous as the Shans,

[1] The information received from Mr. Freeman which is given at the close of this chapter would seem to indicate that

two or three times as many as the Siamese, the Laos constitute the great body of the Tai race. In area of land occupied they are the first among the people of Indo-China; in numbers second only to the Annamites.

Anticipating what will be presented more at length further on, permit the writer to answer in a few words the question, "Why should the Presbyterian Church pray and labor especially for the Laos people?"

First. It is a great field. This requires no further word to one who has read the preceding pages.

Second. It is our field in a sense that can be said of hardly any other great field where our board is at work. Fruitful as has been the missionary work done by our representatives in Canton, China, we share the work and responsibility there with at least four other churches. In Korea, Presbyterians in the United States and in Australia, Northern and Southern Methodists, and a few Anglicans, share with us the responsibility and the blessing. Even in Siam, often spoken of as our field, the Baptists have a small work for the Chinese and the Disciples have opened a station in recent years. Work for the Laos people is wholly our own. A single

the Tai race are more numerous in the north than he had at first supposed. It would appear to be safe to increase the estimate of the total population of the Laos given in the text by at least a million. The Laos probably number from seven to eleven millions.

station of the French Presbyterians in French territory where the French Government at present does not permit us to work, and four hundred miles from our nearest station, is the only exception. The Laos are peculiarly our field.

Third. The Laos are physically vigorous, and rapidly increasing in numbers, and are morally peers of any race in the non-Christian world.

Fourth. Successes already won encourage us to look for still greater fruit in the future. Buddhist peoples are justly regarded as peculiarly difficult to reach with the gospel. The small numbers enrolled in Christian churches among the Burmese, the Ceylonese, the Siamese, after eighty to one hundred years of missionary effort, bear witness to this fact. While the gospel has had no such marvelous success among the Laos as in Korea or the Philippines, we find among them the largest Christian church that has grown up anywhere among the Southern Buddhists.

Fifth. It is a field just now peculiarly open to the gospel. It is a time of transition; never before were the minds of the village and district officials (higher officers are mostly Siamese and comparatively indifferent to religious things), so full of inquiry regarding the ways and religion of the West. In almost every village, in almost every home, the missionary and his message are welcome. The railroad is nearing us, the bicycle and automobile are often seen; the rush of modern life, absorption in material things will within ten years render many of these people more difficult to reach with the gospel. Now is the day of opportunity.

Sixth. It is emphatically a needy field. In a land less densely populated than India or China, the individual missionary can come in touch with only a smaller number. Yet, counting only that part of our field within measurable reach of our present stations, each missionary, clerical or medical, has about him a parish of at least one hundred and fifty thousand souls. Beyond the limits touched in any way by our present work, yet one in blood, in language, in customs, with the Laos of Siam, and equal in population, lie the vast, unoccupied fields of French and Chinese Laos.

"Is the Presbyterian Church planning for anything less than the conquest of the whole Laos people for Christ?"

Since finishing the manuscript of this book, the author has made a journey from Haiphong, in Tonking, to Mengtse, in Yunnan province in China. Returning to Hanoi, he turned northwards and crossed the Chinese border again to Lung-chow, Kwangsi, and from here traveled down the river, via Nanning and Wu-chow, to Hongkong. Writing from Lung-chow, he says that the nearest mission station to the north is Tu-shan-chow, in Kweichow, two hundred and fifty miles distant; to the east, Nanning-fu is one hundred miles in a direct line, or two hundred and fifty miles by the river; due west, the nearest station is Bhamo, seven hundred miles away, although to the northwest there is a station three hundred and fifty miles distant; to the south and west, no Protestant work is found nearer than the Presbyterian station of Chieng Rai, nearly seven hundred miles in a direct line. In this vast area he estimates that there are at least fifteen million people, over five million of whom are of the Tai race. Mr. Freeman writes that he was able to converse with these people with little difficulty, readily understanding five sixths of their words. Of a vocabulary of four hundred words which he gathered on both sides of the Chinese frontier, only sixty-seven, or one in six, differed essentially from the common speech of Chieng Mai, a thousand miles away. There were also slight differences in pronunciation and tone, but the people would soon exclaim, "Why, he speaks Tai." In one village which he visited, the elders gathered and with great cordiality helped him compare their speech with that of Chieng Mai. The vocabulary differed most in religious terms, since the people are not Buddhists.

He closes his letter with this statement of the things accomplished by the journey:

"First. I have succeeded in determining, as no missionary or other traveler has done before, the extent and limits of Tai population and speech. Second, I have found that the Tai people of Tonking, described by French writers who could not speak their language but saw the obvious differences of dress, differ less widely in speech than I expected. In fact, clear over into Kwangtung and Kweichow provinces they are really our people. Third. I have helped to form a bond of Christian fellowship between the churches of Laos and in Kwangsi [where he found churches of Tai blood]. Distant a thousand miles, they are yet kindred in blood as well as in faith. Fourth, I have seen ways in which I hope our own church can immediately and practically help to make a beginning in reaching these brethren of our Laos people with the gospel. I sincerely hope some Laos missionary can come for a year to study the problem and the people more fully than I could do in this hurried journey. He may be able in a year of exploration to help missionaries on the field in Kwangsi to acquire the language of this people, for whom as yet not a single Protestant missionary is definitely at work."

CHAPTER II

SOCIAL CUSTOMS—WOMAN IN THE HOME

Are the Laos Malay or Mongolian? The complexion, physique and industries of the Laos are not unlike those of the Filipinos and other peoples usually accounted Malays; their history and geographical position show close association with the Chinese, and their language, consisting of unchangeable monosyllables, with a highly developed tonal system found outside the Tai race only in China, argues still more definitely for a Mongolian origin. On the other hand, the absence of high cheek bones, almond eyes and the peculiar complexion popularly considered characteristic of the "Yellow Race," has led some students of ethnography to deny that the Laos are Mongolian and even to argue that they are Caucasian. The racial relations of the Laos are puzzling, but the conviction is growing, that the entire Tai race is Mongolian.

Their Race Inheritance But whatever may be the racial relations of the Laos, their social customs, especially the position of women, set them apart for any of their neighbors. Nowhere in Asia, rarely elsewhere, does woman occupy the high place in the home, and

Buddhist Monks

enjoy such entire equality with man before the law, as is accorded to her among the Laos. The Siamese are of kindred blood, but association with other races has modified the position of woman so that she is not the peer of man and the queen of the home among them, as she certainly is among the Laos. This unique position of woman, and the high moral standards that accompany it, cannot be attributed to Buddhism or to any outside influence; they are a part of the racial inheritance of the Laos people.

Laos Courtship

A Laos house consists usually of a single "Roof," somewhat more than half of which is inclosed by walls. Into the inclosed part, the sleeping apartment of the family, the stranger is not invited. The balance, which is inclosed on only two sides, is the living room of the house. Here the family eats and receives guests. On moonlight evenings fathers and mothers who have marriageable daughters retire early, leaving this porch or living room to the young folks. The wall between is thin, usually wickerwork woven of bamboo splints, so that those within can readily hear, even see, if they wish, what goes on. Still the young girl is left largely on her honor, as are American girls in similar circumstances.

Safeguards of Customs

A woman is guarded, however, by custom even more than by the watchfulness of friends. Custom forbids the lover to touch so much as the hand of his mistress, or of any woman. In visiting her, unless he takes a friend with him, he places himself wholly in her power. If she says that in any way he has overstepped the proprieties, no court will listen to his denial. It is assumed that he has offended against the spirits of the household in which he visited, and must pay a fine, the amount of which is determined by custom, to the family of which the girl is a member. It is easy to see how the girl may, and does, abuse this power, but a girl who is known to have done so has few visitors.

Marriage Customs

The parents may arrange a match for son or daughter, but the final decision rests with the girl herself. Not infrequently the young people have their way despite opposition from the parents on one or both sides.

Wedding customs differ widely. Among the poorer people there is often no ceremony and no written contract. The bridegroom simply goes to the home of the bride, and, by becoming a member of his wife's family, ceases to have part or inheritance in his father's family. The inheritance usually, though not necessarily, goes to the daughters and unmarried sons, that is, to those who are resident with the parents at the time of their death. Where either or both parties to the marriage have property, a written legal contract is made, and as a rule there are ceremonies in which the guardian spirits of both households are supposed to take part. So sensitive to ridicule are the contracting parties, however, that the contract is drawn up by the legal representative of each, and the bridegroom usually disappears immediately after the contract has been signed, and is not seen again at the home of the bride for several days. Then the timid husband quietly slips in without remark, and takes up his duties under the critical eyes of his father-in-law and mother-in-law.

Knots Untied

As in western lands, it is not at all uncommon to "marry in haste and repent at leisure." The mother-in-law may conceive a violent dislike to her new son-in-law and tell her daughter to send him packing. The young wife herself may find him lazy or disagreeable, or in a fit of anger she may bundle up his clothes and throw them out of doors. In either case the young man usually stands not on the order of his going. With scarcely more ceremony, he too, may, if he chooses, leave his wife and return to his father's roof. The parents may—often they do—induce the young couple to make up their quarrel, and where property is involved, one or more conferences between the heads of both households is necessary before the separation is complete. Such matters do not often come into the courts.

Divorce Though Easy Not Common

Easy as divorce may seem to be, and loosely as the marriage knot may seem to be fastened in the early years of life together, divorce is not common in later years, and especially after children have been born, unless it be for "statutory cause," which there, as here, is held to dissolve the marriage bond. The injured party may condone the fault, but adultery and polygamy are condemned and forbidden in every form by Laos custom and public opinion. The customs of the Siamese differ radically in these respects from those of the Laos. As Siamese rule and influence have increased in the north, some of the princes and of the official class have taken more than one wife. Siamese law also gives to the husband a license wholly foreign to the purer customs of the Laos.

Famine and Divorce One cause of divorce not uncommon deserves mention, because it shows in a curious way the difference between the point of view of the Laos and our own. Rice is almost the only food of the people. A failure of the rice crop, whether due to drought or flood, means suffering, if not famine, in the region affected by it. Rice may be plenty and cheap forty miles away across the mountains, but the utter lack of roads or good transport facilities makes the suffering acute in the valleys where rice has failed. The father of a family may find that the supply of rice is sufficient to tide wife and children and the wife's parents over until another season, but it is not enough for him also. With the wife's consent he goes across the mountains to seek work and food. He may find both on condition that he marry the daughter of his employer; or for some other reason he may marry there and never return. Does this involve hardship to the wife and children he has left behind? Not necessarily. It must be re-

Laos Women and Children
In Chinese Territory

Laos Women and Children, Chieng Mai

membered that house and farm, cattle and chickens, all he possessed, has been left with the wife.

Parents and Children

The children are not a burden on the mother. At five or six years of age they carry about and amuse a younger brother or sister, help with the wood and water, run errands, and a little later watch the buffaloes and the cattle. The cotton for their scanty clothing is grown, carded, spun and woven with their help in the home. Nearly all they eat is grown in their own field, or garden, or found in the forest. It must not be supposed, however, that the children lack time for merry play, or that their work is constant or beyond their strength.

The Daily Bath

If a young woman is left a widow with small children, this is no bar to remarriage; on the whole, children are regarded as an asset rather than a liability in the land of the Laos. It is a very strong bond which unites parents and children to each other and to the home. Only under most exceptional circumstances, such as famine, does the father leave his wife and children. " Be it ever so humble, there's no place like home," is certainly the sentiment of the Laos. One feature of the home life must not be forgotten. Near the stairs by which one goes up into the house, stands a jar of water and a cocoanut shell dipper. Bare feet are the rule, but if sandals are worn they are removed, and the feet are washed at the jar before entering the house. When the lusty cry of the new-born child is heard, presently the grandmother or some other elderly woman appears and seats herself beside the water jar with the child cradled between her outstretched bare feet. With the cocoanut dipper in her left hand she dashes cold water over the squirming, squealing child, and with her right scrubs it more or less vigorously. Soap is not always used, for soap is a luxury which many cannot afford, so that the missionary has learned that a cake of soap is a most acceptable present. The habit of a daily cold bath thus begun at birth keeps a beautiful, soft glow on the skin of the average Laos man or woman. Whoever among them fails to have his daily bath is uncomfortable. In person and in dress the Laos are a cleanly race.

Daughters

The fact that daughters bring their husbands to live with and so watch over the declining years of father and mother, makes the advent of a girl in the house peculiarly welcome. More than once a father and mother with several stalwart sons have bewailed to me the fact that no daughters have come to bless their home. In such a case one of the sons usually induces his bride to leave her own home and become a daughter to his father and mother, but such an arrangement is contrary to custom (all-powerful among the Laos), difficult for the young woman, and often impracticable, if not impossible.

Woman in the Home

While the wife and mother goes to the early market to sell her produce and buy her supplies, the husband and children get the breakfast and attend to the babies.

Other duties in the home are lighter than in a colder clime. Women, therefore, find time for not a little work out of doors, although the heavier work is always done by the men. The men dig the irrigation ditches, build the dams, plow and harrow the fields. When the land is ready, the wife and children aid in the planting and, later, in the harvest. The lighter work of the garden near the house falls also to the wife and children, and as the garden is made in the dry season, the task of watering and caring for it is not small.

As three fourths of the country is too wild and mountainous ever to be cultivated, and the fertile valleys are usually narrow, the forest is within reach of most villages. Roots and herbs, mushrooms and bamboo shoots found in these forests, frogs and small fish from the streams and ponds, form no small part of the "relish" ("kahp," or "with" is the native word) eaten with rice. Trips to the forest to gather these are a sort of holiday enjoyed and shared in by all the family.

On a Journey

If husband and wife, with or without the children, make a journey together, you will often see the wife carrying some of the products of her garden or loom for sale, or food and other necessities for the journey, the husband striding by her side with little load save his sword and gun. I think this is a reminiscence of a time, not long past, when the men of the party were of necessity free from burdens that they might be on the alert to protect the company from savage beasts and more savage men. Along the more frequented roads and in densely populated regions, especially if there is anything really heavy to be carried, the man usually takes his share of the burden.

Women and Trade

The women rarely share in the longer trading expeditions that make many of the men familiar with the roads for hundreds of miles in every direction from their homes, but the local trade is almost wholly in their hands. Three fourths of the attendants at the daily markets, both buyers and sellers, are women. Most women add not a little to the family income in this way, or by trade in their own homes. The wife is usually the treasurer of the home, and the husband is expected to place his earnings in her hands.

Queen of the Home

In a word, instead of the seclusion or subserviency that is the lot of woman in most parts of Asia, the Laos wife, quite as much as her husband, is the head of the household. Neither the husband nor the wife is expected to enter upon any important business alone. They share the work, the responsibility, the rewards of their labor. The whole atmosphere of a Laos home is on a plane distinctly higher than we find in any other non-Christian land, so far as I am aware. In that home woman is the queen.

CHAPTER III

THE YELLOW ROBE AND WHAT IT BROUGHT TO THE LAOS

The Begging Bowl

As one goes in the early morning along the street of any Laos city or village, he is sure to meet yellow-robed figures with shaven heads. Each carries the "begging bowl" and the fan, characteristic possessions of the Buddhist monk. With the fan he covers his face while he receives gifts of steaming rice at each door and mutters the Buddhist formula of blessing. The wealthier households also send a child or dependent to the monastery loaded with hot food for "the order." In this way every household contributes at least a handful of steaming rice each morning to the support of the monks, and in numberless other ways the rites and observances of which the "Yellow Robe" is the type, touch the daily life and thought of the Laos people.

The Wat, or Temple

About the "wat," which is at once monastery, temple and school, centers the life of the village, of the city, of the whole land. There is the "sala" or rest house where the traveler finds a stopping place; in the "sala," or even in the temple itself, the itinerant trader opens and displays his wares; all the festivals and merrymakings, the social and political, as well as the religious life of the village, there have their homes. It is fair to study first this center of much that appeals to the deepest feelings of the Laos people, and to ask what the Yellow Robe has brought to the Laos.

The Coming of the Yellow Robe

I have already said that, unlike the Siamese and Western Shans, the Laos people came in contact with no other great race in the course of their migration, and were profoundly affected by only one outside influence, that of Buddhism. In Ceylon, Buddhism had retained something of the moral earnestness and missionary spirit that marked its founder. About A. D., 500, a Buddhist revival, begun there, carried the Yellow Robe to Burma and, a little later, to the Laos and Siamese. What did its missionaries bring to this people?

The Laos Alphabet

First. They found the Laos without a written character. With no little ingenuity and patience they adapted the somewhat meager alphabet of Pali, the language of their sacred books, to express the forty-five consonants and forty-four vowels of the Laos tongue, and its eight tones as well. The writer knows of no other alphabet, whether in Europe or in Asia, that is so rich in variety of vocal elements or so competely phonetic as that of the Laos. Yet the task of the Laos child in learning to read is less difficult than that of most European children, far less than that of the English child. The gift of this alphabet, which is popularly believed to have come from the Buddha himself, was not the least of the benefits that Buddhism brought to the Laos.

Buddhism and Education

Second. Buddhism brought also education and the wealth of Indian literature and civilization within the reach of the Laos man. For women, there as everywhere, Buddhism does little. About one in three of the boys is educated in the monasteries. When they have learned to read and to repeat certian formulæ, they may take the first vows as novices. Even if they remain in the temple until they are twenty-one years of age and take the full monastic vows, they are not bound to celibacy and poverty for life. They may leave the order and marry when they choose, and most of them do so. If they have become novices before they leave the monastery, they are known through life by the title of "Noi"; if they have become full monks, they earn the higher title of "Nan." All who have not studied in the monasteries are known as "khone dip," "green men," and readily yield precedence and honor to the "Nan" and the "Noi." Buddhism has made education honorable among the Laos.

The Laos B. A. and M. A.

The Buddhist Bible

The Tri Pitaka, often called the Buddhist Bible, and other books modeled upon it or written about it, constituting the rich and varied literature of Pali Buddhism, are to be found in the original, in whole or part, in many Laos monasteries, but few monks understand them. They have also been rather freely rendered into Laos. The Buddhist canon is not closed as is the canon of our Scriptures; on the contrary, new "scriptures" in the vernacular are still being prepared. They are modeled on the old, and draw largely from them, but they often introduce material entirely unknown to Buddhism a generation ago. For instance, an American missionary found in a monastery in Chieng Mai, a "thum" (sacred book) into which had been woven the story of the creation, the fall, the flood, much as they are found in Genesis, which had then been recently translated into Laos. The monks and abbots seem to make little distinction, as to authority, between the old and the new. Both are read either to gain "merit," or for the stories they contain, rather than for their moral or doctrinal teaching. A considerable literature modeled thus on Buddhist texts has grown up. Folklore tales, plays, poems, conundrums—some original, some derived from India—are found in these books, and are told and retold among the people. Books of proverbs, such as the "Grandfather Teaches His Grandchildren," are deservedly popular, singularly free from anything objectionable, and well worth translation into English.

Laos Vernacular Literature

Laos Minstrelsy

Although a third of the men can read, and crowds gather at the monasteries to listen to the reading of the "thums" or sacred books on Buddhist festival days, the Laos are not a reading people. They would rather listen to a story-teller than read for themselves. Minstrels gifted with facility in extempore verse are in demand on all festal occasions. To the accompaniment of a rude violin, or of a considerable orchestra, they sing the praises of host and guests, whose applause and largesse they constantly win. This gift of minstrelsy belongs rather to the original character of the Laos, than to anything that has come to them from without, but it has grown and developed with the intellectual development of the people.

What Is Buddhism?

Thus the educational influence of Buddhism upon the Laos has been great and beneficent. But what shall we say of Buddhism as a philosophy, a moral and religious system? This question is more difficult to answer. Sakya Muni, the Buddha (or "enlightened one"), was first of all a philosopher who sought the cause and cure of evil. His answer to the great problem of the world is found in his system of asceticism which aims to extinguish both desire and regret, both joy and sorrow, and ultimately to lose personal existence in Nirvana. It denies the existence of the soul, and teaches nothing of God. Arising out of a protest against the polytheism of India, it was accused of atheism, and this accusation can hardly be denied. Although Buddhism does not actually deny the existence of God, or of gods, it ignores them, it does not

An Atheistic Philosophy

worship them. It is practically atheism. The Buddha was but a man and has ceased to be; so their own books say. The Buddhist is not taught to lift the soul to anything above man himself.

Karma and Rebirth

The idea of birth and death and rebirth, sometimes as an animal, again as man or angel, seems strange to a western mind, but had and has great hold on the thought of India. While transmigration seems utterly at variance with his denial of personality and of soul, Sakya Muni accepted it in a modified form, the doctrine of "Karma." Few even of the followers of the Buddha understand, or pretend to understand, his meaning. The idea commonly current among them is akin rather to the cruder ideas of transmigration current in India. I shall therefore not attempt to explain "Karma," but only refer to literature on that subject.[1] In some form,

[1] According to Buddhist psychology there is no personal soul, but only a union of qualities which are in a constant state of change. To use an illustration: no single kind of building material constitutes a house, nor all of them merely gathered together. They may form a house, but it is nothing apart from them and when they are taken away there is no house left. In like manner the union of qualities constitutes the individual, but when they are dissolved there is nothing left. The way in which they have interacted during life, however, creates "Karma," merit or desert. In accordance with this a new individual is formed after death by a regrouping of the qualities. This new individual has not the same personality as the old, for there is no such thing as personality; but his condition depends on the Karma or merit of the former individual.—Ed.

belief in transmigration has firm hold on the minds of the Laos people.

Merit-Making That every good deed has for its object to gain merit for the doer, is the firm conviction of every Buddhist. Real altruism, action prompted by love for one's fellow rather than by ultimate gain to one's self, is not expected outside the family circle, nor is it understood. If a man gives alms, he does it to accumulate merit that shall ultimately outweigh his demerit, and promote his own happiness hereafter. If he builds a monastery, or makes gifts to the "order," or places a jar of water by the roadside that the weary traveler may drink, he makes merit thereby. To place a son, a grandson or some other lad in the monastery and support him there, to make the customary offerings and meet the other expenses involved in his entrance into the "order," is a common form of "merit-making."

Gala Days The gala days of the year are those on which the people of a village unite to "make merit" by offerings at the common sanctuary. These "merit-makings" are the occasion of no little rivalry in display and taste, not merely in the number and beauty of the offerings, but in the design and construction of the "sadees," or miniature temples and palaces in which the gifts are carried to the temples. Rivalry and the desire for display, rather than any religious motive, is behind many of the gifts. Yet the aged especially, realizing that their time for "merit-making" is limited, and knowing no other way to win favor in the unknown land from which no traveler returns, often make sacrifices that are pathetic.

The Ten Commandments of Buddha

The "Ten Precepts" of Sakya Muni have often been compared with the Ten Commandments of Moses. Like the Ten Commandments, the "Ten Precepts" are divided into two tables, of which this is the first:

Do not take life whether of man or beast.
Do not take what is not given.
Abstain from unlawful sexual intercourse.
Do not lie.
Do not drink wine or strong drink.

These correspond somewhat closely to the second half of the decalogue, and are recognized as binding on the laity as well as on the monks.

The first half of the decalogue of Moses has to do with our duties to God, and finds no parallel whatever in the "Ten Precepts," the second half of which is as follows:

Do not eat at forbidden times.
Abstain from dancing, singing, music and stage plays.
Use not a high or broad bed.
Take not pleasure in garlands, scents or ornaments.
Receive not silver or gold.

It is evident that these latter precepts apply only to the monks, bidding them carry out the monastic ideas of Sakya Muni. The casual visitor at the "wats" will soon discover that little real effort is made to obey them.

How is it with the first half of the "Precepts"? While offenses and evasions constantly occur, (offenses against the precepts occur in the monasteries, as well as outside), yet dishonesty, drunkenness and impurity are certainly less rife among the Laos than in other parts of Asia. The scandals so commonly connected with Buddhist temples in China, Korea and Japan, and so inseparable from Brahman worship in India, are practically unknown in Laos temples.

Buddha's Greatest Command

One precept demands especial mention, the first and great command of the Buddha, "Do not take life whether of man or beast." The more conscientious monks strain all the water they drink; they go so far as to step aside from the path rather than crush an ant or worm. Even the common people count the fisherman or hunter a constant offender against Buddhist law. The fisherman feels that he evades the law if he allows the fish he has caught to die of itself, as it soon will. The priests themselves constantly eat the flesh of animals some one else has killed. So long as he does not actually take life, the Laos man counts cruelty to animals no offense against this law. He may maim or torture them, or look on suffering with seeming utter indifference. A law intended to develop pity has worked rather the other way. He considers it impossible to keep the law, for there, as everywhere, man craves flesh food. However, the fact that Christianity specifically sanctions the use of flesh as food, thus releasing him from bondage to a law he cannot keep, appeals to the common sense of every Laos man as an argument for Christianity. So does also the statement of Scripture that man, unlike the beast, is made in the image of God.

The Messianic Hope of Buddhism

It is not unfair to say that Buddhism is not in the deeper sense a religion. It gives little or nothing to satisfy the real cravings of the human heart. One thing, however, it does give which ought not to be omitted in any statement of Laos Buddhism: When the older men and women go to the temples on the Buddhist sacred days they are wont to pray that their life may be prolonged until they shall "see the face of him that is to come." They say that the Buddha told his followers that he, himself, was not a saviour, but that in the future there will come another "enlightened one," who shall save all that shall behold his face. I am told that this vivid sense of a messiah that is to come is not found among the Burmese and other Buddhists. Be that as it may, the impression made by this hope upon the Laos gives to the messenger of Christ an opportunity much used by our evangelists, to present to them Jesus as the one who fulfills the hope of all nations.

The Arts in Laos Temples

The architecture of the Laos may be mainly borrowed from India and Burma, and its art as displayed in the images and pictures in its temples may be somewhat crude, yet the fact remains that Buddhism brought these arts to the Laos and that the boys in the temple schools learn not merely to read, but to saw lumber, to make brick and mortar, to build with brick as well as wood, to manufacture the umbrellas, the fans and many other articles they constantly use. We have seen reason to attribute to earlier causes rather than to Buddhism the comparatively high moral standards of the Laos, and that religion did little to develop the spiritual side of man's nature; but, even so, it still would be difficult to exaggerate the importance of Buddhism in the life of the people. Much that is best in their language and literature, the very characters in which it is written, they owe to Buddhism; much of their knowledge of the arts and of civilization came to them with the Yellow Robe. Buddhism found the Laos, as Christianity found our ancestors about the same time, little above the status of the savage; it has made education honorable and strengthened and conserved the moral standards it found already among them. When we compare it with the other religions of Asia, even with so-called Christianity as we find it in South America, in Mexico and in the Philippines, we must concede that Buddhism has given much that is good, little that is evil to the Laos.

The Debt of the Laos to Buddhism

CHAPTER IV

DEMON WORSHIP AND WITCHCRAFT

The Laos Boatmen

In the crowded harbor and waterways of Bangkok, the traveler watches with curiosity the Laos boats and boatmen. The craft are ill adapted to deep-water navigation; the navigators are out of their element on the sea. But see them rather in the roaring rapids of the Me Ping, down which, under their steady hands and eyes the boats dash safely, yet almost at railway speed. In August, 1908, the writer raced down these thirty-two rapids, a distance of at least eighty miles, in seven hours. He has shot the Sault Ste. Marie in an Indian canoe, and found it hardly more thrilling, and while the passage of the Sault is over in five minutes, the rapids of the Me Ping continue with brief intervals of more quiet water for a whole day. The beetling cliffs, the swirling waters, the erect, alert boat captain, grasping with firm hand the giant steering oar, giving at just the right moment a few powerful strokes—it is a picture one can never forget. The writer is proud to call some of these boatmen his friends, men of splendid physique, accustomed to meet and overcome danger in many forms.

Me Ping Rapids

River Superstitions

Yet the very dangers that surround and the firm belief that the rapids of the Me Ping are the abode of spirits that lie in wait for the unwary, make the Laos boatmen, like the deep-sea fishermen of Labrador, exceedingly superstitious. For instance: we are started for the long trip of seven hundred miles to Bangkok. We tie up for the night at a village where some of the boatmen live.

The next morning breakfast time passes and there are no signs of departure. "What is the trouble, captain?" "Two of the men have gone to have their grandfather tie their wrists," is the answer. Later in the day two hours more are spent at another village that another boatman may be similarly protected from the dangers that await us. At the head and again at the foot of the rapids, the boatmen stop to make offerings to the spirits.

Spirit Worship

Not only the boatmen, but the whole land and the whole people, are full to overflowing with customs and practices prompted by belief in unseen powers constantly ready to work them harm. As we travel by land, we often come to rude shrines where travelers offer flowers and food to the unseen powers. At night, as we camp in the forest, some of the men probably make such an offering before they taste their evening meal. Before they plant their rice, the villagers unite in offering chickens, or a pig, to the spirits of the fields. Some especially curious superstitions gather about the building of the house. No Laos man, not a Christian, would venture to take parts of two houses to build one, nor to use in any way the charred posts or beams of a house that has been injured by fire. Lucky days and hours must be chosen for any important undertaking. When sickness and death come, more sinister forms of the spirit superstition are sure to multiply. The new-born babe is laid across the head of the steps with an adjuration to the demons that, if the babe be the child of the spirits, the spirit will take it now; if not, that it be left forever alone. About the last rites for the dead and the place of burial superstition again gathers. From childhood to old age the fear of evil spirits is ever present, a bondage all feel and would shake off if they could.

Benign Spirits

The Laos people recognize the existence of benign spirits who have an influence over their destinies. One old lady, whom it was a pleasure to visit, repeated to me a prayer not unlike the "Now I lay me" of our childhood days, with which each evening she committed herself to the care of these good spirits. But such worship of good spirits is unusual; spirit worship as we usually find it is directed to the evil spirits, and prompted wholly by fear. It is difficult to get at the real thought of the people, for they recognize that such worship is evil and are ashamed of it while they cling to it.

Buddhism and Spirit Worship

Buddhism, the nominal religion of the Laos, absolutely forbids any worship of the evil spirits. "Make not the spirits great; he who makes the spirits great, whether by tying the wrist, or wearing charms, or tattooing charms, by feeding the spirits or making offerings to them, that man is outside the religion of Gautama." These are quoted as the words of the Buddha himself. Yet all the Laos people worship the spirits, and the Buddhist monks themselves are very often the leaders in this worship.

How shall we explain this total disregard of Buddha's express command? Why has Buddhism failed to drive out the demon worship that here, as all over Asia, preceded it?

Unable to Supplant It. Why?

First. Because spirit worship has always entered more deeply into the life and soul of the Laos people than Buddhism. Their sense of the presence and influence of the unseen has only been dulled, never removed, by Buddhist teachings. Though the Laos seek merit by listening to the Buddhist scriptures, and repeating its formulæ of devotion; though the men are educated in Buddhist monasteries, and the women seek favor by supporting a son or grandson in the priesthood; though the whole social life of the people centers in the Buddhist "wat" or monastery; still spirit worship is to-day, as it ever has been, the real religion of the Laos people.

No Power to Deliver

Second. Because, while the Buddha saw that the worship of evil spirits was wrong and useless, while he himself may have broken with it wholly, he gave to his followers no refuge or strength that could deliver them from the fear of the unseen. Ask a Laos man why he worships the spirits, and if he answers at all, he will say it is because he dare not omit it. As the spirits said to the sons of Sceva, as recorded in the book of Acts, "Jesus I know, and Paul I know; but who are ye?" So demon worship in Asia has in effect said to Buddhism, "Who are ye?"

Buddhism has in it no power to deliver its followers from the spirits. It has practically surrendered to the demons all they claim. The Buddhist monasteries are to-day, at least in many cases, the centers of the demon worship, and the bondage of the people to fear continues to-day as before the "Yellow Robe" came to them.

Christ and the Demons

Demon worship in itself is always and everywhere a thing to be pitied and deplored. Yet in its relation to the work of the Christian missionary, even demon worship may be a schoolmaster to lead to Christ, for it has served to keep alive in the minds and hearts of the Laos people a sense of the unseen, a realization that man is dependent on spiritual powers outside himself for safety, for help, for his very being. I doubt whether it can be said that the Laos people worship or distinctly recognize a supreme being. The names of Phya Phom and Phya In (Brahm and Indra of Indian mythology) are often on their lips in folklore tales derived from India, but I do not think either is recognized as supreme, nor are prayers or worship directed to them so far as I am aware. Still, there is everywhere prevalent a sense of dependence on unseen spiritual powers, wholly foreign to the self-dependence, the atheism, of Buddhism.

Christus Liberator

No stories from the Bible so readily hold the attention of a Laos audience as those of the creation and of the power of Christ over the demons. A God who created all and has power to deliver from evil spirits, meets the need and longing of their hearts. Many of our Christian people have thus been first drawn to Christ. While they continue to believe that evil spirits are about them on every hand, they believe that Jesus has delivered them from their power, and that in his name they can defy and cast them out. Even of those who have not accepted Christ, multitudes recognize that over those who have accepted him, the demons have no power.

Prince and Peasant

Kindred with the spirit worship is the universal belief in witchcraft. An account of the first case that came under the writer's own observation will show better than any description the power and bearing of this delusion.

Nan Teo was a well-to-do Laos farmer in a village twenty miles from the city of Nan. He had a good rice field, buffaloes (used in plowing), several cattle, and a well-built house. A petty prince or "chow," who lived near him, wanted his field, but Nan Teo refused to sell. Nominally, a "man of the people" has just the same rights before the law as a hereditary prince; practically, a man who opposes a "chow" has little chance of success. We shall see that Nan Teo found this out to his cost.

The Spirit Doctor

Not long after after Nan Teo's refusal to sell, a man in his village became seriously ill. The spirit doctor was, of course, consulted, and he declared at once that the spirits of some one were making all the trouble. He proceeded to stick pins into the body of the sick man who was already delirious, and to scarify his flesh with a tiger's tooth, so that his delirious cries, commonly believed to be the cries of the spirit that possessed him, might reveal the identity of the witch. The witch doctor soon interpreted these incoherent cries as an accusation against Nan Teo's wife and mother.

The Accusation

So deep-rooted is the witchcraft superstition in the minds of the Laos people that the victim often acquiesces in the penalty inflicted, believing that even unconsciously he is responsible in some way for the illness or death of the patient. In this case Nan Teo's wife and mother indignantly denied the accusation, believing, as they afterwards told me, that the witch doctor was in the pay of the "chow" who wanted to buy their field.

The Penalty In some way, evidence satisfactory to the minds of the superstitious village elders was obtained, and they insisted that the accused were guilty. The whole family was ordered to leave the village. They demurred and delayed, hoping at least to get a fair price for their belongings. An offer made for their cattle was far below what they were worth, and they refused it. That night one of the cattle was ruined by a sword cut. The next day they agreed to sell, and the "chow" promised to pay them about half what their field was worth. As yet, no money had been paid in either case, but the limit of time set for them to leave the village had come. In the night while they were asleep, some one set fire to their house and they escaped with only the clothes on their backs and what they could carry in their hands.

Flight and Despair The next night the missionary found the whole family of five shivering over a scanty fire at a "rest house" near his own door, and not far from the city of Nan. They had neither food, nor blankets, nor money. Bit by bit he drew from them their pitiful story, and with the coöperation of the native Christians relieved their immediate necessities. He gave them a place to stay and work so that they could maintain themselves, and a promise to help them collect the money due them. I left not long afterwards, and I do not know whether they succeeded in collecting the price of their field and cattle. I doubt whether they did, unless through the influence of the foreigner.

Results The members of this family were intelligent and industrious, and so far as we could ascertain, had never before had any trouble with their neighbors. Yet in a week's time, by working on the superstitions of the villagers, the "chow" had deprived them of home and farm and all that they had, and turned them out, houseless and penniless wanderers. Such accusations are less frequent and less effectual now than in the past, but in a dozen years in Laos land I have known personally of many cases. Sometimes the accusations are directed against those who have made themselves obnoxious to the village; sometimes, as in the case cited, personal jealousy, covetousness or spite seems at work. Sometimes, at least, all parties concerned really believe the accused are possessed by, or in league with, evil spirits.

The writer has never seen a case of "spirit possession" that seemed to him real; other intelligent observers recognize the reality of it, at least in some cases. Yet, to argue against spirit possession with a Laos man or woman would be a waste of breath.

"Spirit People" The "spirit people," that is those who have been driven away from their own villages through accusations of witchcraft, do not readily find a home in other villages, or even in the distant parts of the province. Their reputation is almost sure to go with them or follow them. Out in the mountains or forests, away from villages, there are whole villages of these "spirit people," where they have begun life anew, hoping to be free from persecution. As a whole, the people of such a village are apt to be below the average in intelligence and thrift, but discouragement and adverse circumstances account for this in part. Not a few of our most active and self-helpful Christian families have come from those who, at some time, were accused of witchcraft.

The Missionary's Opportunity

Where the missionary or native Christians have been able to show kindness to these accused persons in the time of their distress, they have often shown the deepest gratitude and have readily accepted the invitation to attend Christian services and read Christian books. Gradually the conviction that Christ is more powerful than the demons, that Christians need not and do not fear them, has gained currency among the people, non-Christian as well as Christian. They see, too, that "spirit people" who have become Christians are no longer a danger to their neighbors. It has, therefore, become rather common for a family accused or suspected of witchcraft to invite the elders or leaders of the nearest group of Christians to come and hold service in their house, and to tear down at the same time the charms and spirit shrines that are a mark of all non-Christian homes. By this act they declare to all the village that they are Christians. Often, though not always, there is an end of accusation and suspicion. We accept such people as catechumens, but are slow to receive them to full membership in our churches, until a consistent Christian life for at least a year testifies to the reality of the change in allegiance.

The Outlook Gradually the power of the witchcraft superstition is being broken. The manifest use made of it by designing men to promote their ends, as in the case of Nan Teo, has weakened its hold upon the more intelligent of the people. Progress in intelligence and education works against it; the spread of Christianity has weakened its hold on all who recognize Christ's power, whether they personally accept him or not. Yet the belief of most earnest Christian workers in spirit possession among those who have not taken "refuge with Christ," still continues. In these and in other forms, belief in spirits and worship of them continues to be the real religion of the Laos people.

CHAPTER V

ARTS AND INDUSTRIES

The Average Man

Silk and cotton fabrics as delicately fine, silver and gold as intricately wrought, ivory as beautifully carved as the marts of India afford, are not to be found among the Laos. Their lacquer is less beautifully finished, and their pottery is rude, as compared with the products of Japan and China. But the average Laos man lives in a better house and is more cleanly and better clothed and fed, than the average man on the plains of India. He is not only skillful in the use of his own tools, but ready to devise or adopt new tools, new expedients, new methods.

Home Industries

As in the homes of our grandfathers in pioneer days, many a Laos home produces, not only its own food, but its own clothing. It depends also on the labor of members of the household for building material of every sort, even for most of its tools and utensils. In cities and large villages many foreign goods are sold, but in the more remote villages many a household is clad in the product of its own cotton field and loom, eats little it does not raise or gather in the forest, uses few tools or utensils not made under its own roof, and thus is dependent upon the outside world for little except salt and the iron from which their tools are forged or cast.

A Laos Village

In less isolated places, division of labor has gone farther. Almost every villager above the average in intelligence has some specialty that occupies his time when field or herd do not require attention. One is skillful in weaving baskets or matting, another makes better hats than his neighbors, a third is a blacksmith, a fourth excels in silver and brass work. This woman is a skillful trader and invests her capital in pepper, salt, or limes, when they are plenty; in the house opposite the women spend most of their time at their looms; others give time and strength to gardens of peppers, cotton, onions and tobacco. Weaving and the other processes that intervene between cotton boll or silkworm cocoon and the finished garment, have ever been looked on as peculiarly woman's work. Nowhere are to be found cotton goods of firmer texture, or with colors more cunningly blended, than on the looms of a Laos household. Beautiful silks are also woven, especially in Nan province. Though flax is raised, it is used only for cordage, and in making seines and nets.

A Worthy Woman

As I watch the better class of Laos women in their work, I am often reminded of Solomon's description of a worthy woman in the last chapter of Proverbs: "She seeketh wool and flax, and worketh willingly with her hands. . . . She layeth her hands to the distaff, and her hands hold the spindle. . . . She maketh linen garments and selleth them, and delivereth girdles unto the merchant." "She considereth a field, and buyeth it; with the fruit of her hands she planteth a vineyard. . . . She looketh well to the ways of her household, and eateth not the bread of idleness." (Part of Prov. 31:13-27.) Evidently times and circumstances when these words were written were in some respects not unlike those of the Laos people to-day.

Mechanical Ingenuity Not all the credit in textiles, however, is due the women. The cotton gin, the spinning wheels, the reels and the shuttles, as well as the loom itself, are made by the men. It is worthy of note, too, that the looms are more substantial and more convenient than those in common use in Burma, India and China. The ingenuity displayed in the loom appears also in the plow. We have all seen pictures of the plows in common use in some parts of Asia, very rude and inefficient; the Laos farmer uses a plow with a well-made iron share, well adapted to his needs. Again, since iron is costly and cannot be used freely in house-building, many houses are put together with wooden pins; perhaps there is not a nail in the whole structure. To make places for these pins a good auger is a necessity, and Laos ingenuity has devised one. With a native hatchet, a large and a small knife, chisels and planes of his own manufacture, a saw and a gimlet, a Laos carpenter will turn out cabinetwork that would puzzle an American master carpenter with a full chest of tools. With a bit of bamboo, a rope and a few odd pieces of wood, he will improvise a lathe that does excellent work. The mechanical skill that enables him to make good use of his own tools, makes him equally ready to use better tools when he can get them. Laos artisans to-day are demanding the very best wood-working tools, and they are willing to pay for them. But what has most impressed me as I have worked with them is their readiness of resource, and mechanical gift that, if it cannot do a thing in an accustomed way, will devise some way to reach the result.

The Building of the House

Almost every Laos man can plan and build his own house and fashion some, at least, of the ruder tools he needs on his farm and in his home. Some one in every village can boss the job of sawing any lumber he may need. With a piece of hoop iron, a file, and wood that is at hand, he will make the saw he needs. Better saws can now be had of German make, and many are sold, but much lumber is still sawed, and well sawed, with the rudest tools.

The frame of a Laos house is like the frame our grandfathers made, a few heavy timbers mortised together instead of many smaller ones. The walls are paneled like a door, and are completed ready to set in place before the "house-raising" begins. Posts, sills, plates and rafters, the entire frame is carefully fitted together, piece by piece, and carefully numbered, bamboo for the floors and thatch for the roofs are also ready, and a pig and other supplies for the feast as well. The lucky day is determined upon, and all the village is invited to the "raising." Work often begins before it is really light, for it would be ill luck if even a post hole were dug the day before; material may all be ready, but the actual work of erecting the house must be completed in a day. Many hands make light work of the heaviest tasks, and a small house is often completed before noon.

The House-Raising Feast

The women of the house and of the neighborhood have not been idle in the meantime. The pig has been killed and great quantities of rice, peppers, bananas and vegetables provided. About eight in the morning, and again in the middle of the day, the merry work ceases, and all gather about the tiny round tables with their steaming loads of rice and curry. At "house-raisings," as on other gala occasions, the feast is an indispensable part of the ceremonies, and if the work continues until night, feasting and merry-making, too often quickened by liberal use of the native rice whiskey, may continue till the wee small hours.

Betel-Chewing

Cigarettes, or tobacco to make them, "meeung," or wild tea leaves and the betel tray, are all passed around after the more substantial part of the feast is over. A child, four or five years old, imitates his elders, and is found gravely lighting his cigarette, or busily chewing his "meeung" or betel nut. Betel-chewing is not peculiar to Siam, but is a custom common in India, Burma and China, as well. A fresh sera leaf, a dab of lime paste, a bit each of betel nut, of tobacco and of an astringent bush, all wrapped in the sera leaf, form the quid, and every man as he returns to work carries such a quid very evidently in one cheek. Betel-chewing tends to blacken the teeth and stain the lips and tongue a brick red. It also tends to make the gums recede from the teeth till the latter are loose and ready to drop out before old age fairly approaches. Still the "chew" of betel is antiseptic and helps to preserve the teeth even while it blackens them. Disgusting as the habit and the results are to us, more can be said in its favor than appears at first sight.

Signs of Prosperity

Houses may be built almost wholly of bamboo, but such a house lasts at most only a few years, and more often posts and frames are of solid wood. Given a frame of native "mahogany" that will last a lifetime, if the family prospers basket work gives place in the walls to teak or oil-wood panels; sawed lumber replaces bamboo planks in the floor; and a tile roof takes the place of thatch. The transformation may be gradual, but it is typical of the change that I have watched over the whole land the past fifteen years. Though timber is more expensive and labor

THE KING'S TEMPLE, CHIENG MAI

better paid, every year has seen improvement in the character of the houses built. It has been said, with some truth, I think, that if a Burman or a Siamese gets money ahead, it generally goes onto his back or into his belly; but the Laos man's first thought is a better house.

Temple Architecture

The art and architectural skill of the Laos still center where they began, in the Buddhist monasteries and temples. Only these and city walls have in the past been built of brick. Indeed, I am told that an old superstition forbade the use of brick in other ways. If so, the power of that superstition is gone; public buildings, public stores, even dwelling houses are to-day being built of brick. Yet the temples are still the most imposing and attractive buildings. In the city as well as in the village, sometimes in the midst of a forest or on top of a commanding hill, their many-storied, pagoda-like roofs (see accompanying picture of a temple in Chieng Mai) attract and hold the eye. This heavy roof does not rest on the brick walls alone, but on beautiful wooden columns, such as appear in the temple interior on the same page. On these columns, as well as on the entrance doorway, or the whole front, a wealth of decoration in carving, lacquer and gold leaf, often most effective, is laid with a lavish hand. The pagodas found within the areas of all important temples are unlike the many-storied pagodas of China. Like many other features of the temples, they mark the dependence of Laos builders on

Indian models. Some recent temples follow Burmese models, but the result is usually less pleasing than the older work. Thousands of dollars are spent each year in gold leaf to cover afresh the ancient pagodas that mark places held peculiarly sacred. The great pagoda in Lampoon, one of the ancient capitals, has been twice completely regilded in the ten years of my residence there. The increase in wealth and population that has accompanied peace, has been in no way more distinctly marked than by the increasing number and beauty of the temples.

City Walls

Laos city walls are often substantial and picturesque. Of no avail against modern artillery, they were a real protection against robber raids such as were common scarce forty years ago. Built usually of brick over earth, the presence of laterite blocks in some of them, as at Lampoon, indicates that in part, at least, those walls go back hundreds of years. Stone masonry, now apparently a lost art among the Laos, seems to have been then fairly common. However, stone well adapted to masonry is neither abundant nor easily accessible to the cities.

About twenty walled cities still exist in the Laos states of Siam alone. The number of ruined cities is much larger, but this does not so much imply that the population was at times larger than now, as that in those troublous times one city after another was taken and destroyed, and if rebuilt, rebuilt on a new site rather than on the old. In recent years part of these walls, especially the curious "pig's ear" outworks at the city gates, have been pulled down, and the material used in road-making. Still, much that is picturesque remains, though the growth of the cities to-day is mainly outside the walls.

The Lacquer Industry

One of the most curious and important industries of the Laos is the manufacture of lacquer ware. From Chieng Mai this ware is not only sent all over the Laos states, but to Bangkok as well. Anyone who compares the Laos ware with Japanese or Russian lacquer ware, will be struck at once with its extreme lightness. If he examines carefully, and finds some nick in the lacquer covering, he may discover the reason; the Laos lacquer is laid over an exceedingly fine and strong basket work of split bamboo. While its finish is less artistic than the Japanese ware, its lightness, its strength, and its graceful form commend it to all. The gum from which the lacquer is prepared is found in the Laos forests, and forms an important article of export.

Laos Silverware

Repoussé work in silver and gold is done with much skill in all Laos cities, but little of this work has found its way to foreign markets. This is because Burmese silver work is similar and equally good, and there is in the Laos states no adequate supply of native silver. However, some exquisite specimens of silverware and ivory carving have recently drawn attention to it. There is a little brass and no gold in the country, save what is imported, and work in these metals is not important. Charcoal, iron and steel of fair quality are made and wrought into knives, plowshares and other utensils and tools, but the supply is inadequate, and there is a considerable demand for foreign iron and ironware. No coal has yet been found, and iron is not abundant, so the industrial future is not promising. Laos will never be a rich country.

Carving and Sculpture

No notice of Laos industries should fail to mention wood-carving, as no Laos temple, or Laos house of any pretensions, would be complete without it. Even in the humbler homes and humblest utensils, exquisite bits of the wood-carver's art are often found. The gable ends, the ridgepole, lintel and doorposts, the doors themselves, the entire front of the temple sometimes, are adorned with carvings in teak wood, sometimes covered with lacquer and inlaid with mother-of-pearl. It is less perfect than the best Swiss and Tyrolese carving, but one is often reminded of these. Finely carved images of the Buddha in rock crystal are found in some of the older temples, as well as images in bronze, brass and silver, but I do not know that such work is produced to-day. The most common images and ornamental work in the temple are of brick covered with stucco. The best work of this sort to-day is done by men who have learned their trade in Burma. However, the amount of stucco work is everywhere so great that much of it must

A Laos Boat
Note Polemen and Cabin

be native. Some of it is very effective. Stucco work as well as wood-carving and brass work in the temples are often covered with gold leaf. Princes and wealthy merchants thus display their wealth, and gain, as they think, much merit for themselves.

Boat-Building Laos boats are of a peculiar type, and are specially fitted to the water they have to navigate. Of too shallow draft and too small freight capacity for the lower river, they seem odd and out of place in Bangkok. It is when poled or pulled up the swirling waters of the rapids that they may be seen at their best. The building of these boats is one of the main industries at Chieng Mai and river villages near by. A single tree trunk forty or fifty feet long is hollowed out, then gradually spread by steam and pressure to form not only the keel, but two feet of the sides. Above this the sides are formed of planks, lap-streaked on. The deck, the walls and roof of the cabin, the high prow, the enormous steering oar, all have a history and a peculiar adaptation to needs. The stern, shaped like a fish's tail, seems merely ornamental, but may have a use a foreigner does not readily understand. The keel and bottom, all of one piece, is exceedingly heavy, but it makes the boat rigid and specially fits it to be dragged safely over the rocks that fill the narrow channel at the rapids in low water.

Already the railway is surveyed to Lakawn, and in ten years from now the Laos boat may be a thing of the past, and one of the most picturesque elements in Laos life may disappear forever.

Inroads of Civilization

As in other parts of Asia, the conventional garb and utilitarian ways of the West are gradually replacing the distinctive dress, utensils and conveyances of oriental peoples. Western civilization brings advantages to the East that I do not mean to minimize, but it is robbing it, as it has already robbed the West, of much that is picturesque and in the highest sense useful.

CHAPTER VI

THE LAOS YEAR IN FIELD AND HARVEST

Rice and Teak

Rice and teak may seem to have little in common, but for the Laos man they fit into one another both in space and time. One furnishes his main food, the other his main source of wealth; one keeps him busy in the wet season, the other in the dry; one occupies the plain, the other the mountain and forest. To these two great industries of rice-growing and lumbering all others are subordinate and secondary. If you would know and appreciate Laos industry and life, you must see it in rice-planting and harvest, in logging camp and river jam.

Rainfall and Rice

The planting and care of the rice crop among the hills of the north is by no means so simple a matter as on level plains near the sea. There the Burmese or Siamese farmer simply waits until the abundant rains flood the whole country, and keep it flooded through the rice season. Not so in the north, where lofty ranges of mountains along the Burmese border rob the trade winds of most of the burden of rain they bring from the Bay of Bengal before they reach the plains of northern Siam. Along the western side of these mountains from

Maulmein in Burma, north to Assam, an annual rainfall of one hundred and twenty to two hundred and forty-five inches makes irrigation unnecessary. As one goes south from Maulmein, the mountains are lower and cut off less rain, so that nearly the same conditions prevail in lower Siam. On the other hand, in Chieng Mai the total rainfall does not usually exceed forty inches, and is much less regular. The Laos farmer must therefore depend for his rice crop, not on the irregular rainfalls in the plains, but on the mountain streams.

Irrigation Irrigation is a necessity and a problem of serious difficulty. When one sees great ditches that bring the water many miles, with aqueducts that carry them at times across not inconsiderable valleys and streams, and realizes that all this work has been done without transit or compass, or other surveying instruments; when one sees the dams and levees that are built to control the floods, and watches the teak logs whirled end over end against these feeble barriers by the swollen waters, he begins to appreciate the patience and skill of the Laos farmer. At best the ditches must be cleansed of accumulated sediment each season, the aqueducts and dams repaired and strengthened or rebuilt each year, and only constant watchfulness in flood time can save the levees and dams from destruction, the crops from serious loss. All this work, too, is done by hand; no scrapers or ditchers, or pile-drivers help in the work, which is usually done by the families whose rice plains "eat" the water of the ditch in question. Despite their efforts, not unfrequently the teak logs that beat like battering rams against dam and dike in flood time break through the one or the other, and whether the supply of water is thus cut off from the higher levels, or the lower levels inundated thereby, in either case the crop is ruined. The rice farmer's lot is not an easy one.

Rice Field and Plow

The whole area fed by a ditch is terraced and divided by narrow ridges of earth that serve as footpaths when the plain is flooded, into sections usually less than a quarter of an acre in size, each of which must be perfectly level. The water is allowed to enter the higher terraces first, then, as a section or terrace is flooded, the water is turned to other and lower ones. When a section has been flooded, so that the hard-baked earth has become soft, plowing begins. The plowshare is not unlike one share of an old-fashioned "double-shovel plow" or a corn cultivator, but when set at the proper angle and skillfully handled it turns the earth, now softened by the overflow, almost as well as our own plows, but does not go as deep.

The Water Buffalo

As in the Philippines and in India, the animal that draws the plow is the clumsy-looking water buffalo. His big body and horns and short legs give a false impression; usually slow and sleepy in his movements, his eyes watch everything, and when aroused he is capable of considerable speed and is a fierce antagonist. He is a more real and present danger to the traveler than the tiger that lurks in the forest. Yet dangerous as he is, he is often curiously docile in the hands of the tiny boy or girl who watches him. Enormously heavy and strong, fond of the water and mud in which he delights to wallow, he is just fitted to pull the plow and harrow in the flooded rice fields. There the buffalo is always used singly. They are yoked in pairs to haul timber and logs. The buffalo is used for about three hours in the early morning, and again in the cool of the evening, but from eight to four—through the heat of the day—he must be allowed to rest and feed. If he cannot find mud in which to wallow, or a stream in which to lie while he chews his cud, he does not thrive. At night, tethered together in the dooryard, the animals edge up to the smudge that is built to keep off the mosquitoes.

Rice-Planting

The water is allowed to stand on the plowed fields until grass and weeds are in a measure killed, then a peculiar harrow, drawn by a buffalo—not unlike an old-fashioned hayrake—drags out the weeds and straw and at the same time mixes the mud and water to a tolerably smooth mass. In the middle of the day, while the buffalo rests and feeds, the farmer is busy completing by hand the work of the harrow, repairing the ridges of earth that confine the water to each section, and controlling the flow of water.

Meantime the seed rice has been thickly sown in beds where the children can watch it and keep off the crows. I know of no more beautiful sight than the fresh green of these seed beds in which the rice is allowed to grow until it is about a foot high. It is then pulled up, shaken from the earth, and tied in bunches convenient for handling.

Plowing and harrowing are now completed, and earth and water over the flooded fields form a creamy paste of mud, in which father and mother wade while they plant the rice. Holding in the left hand a bunch of the young rice, with the right each deftly seizes two spears of rice and plunges them together into the soft mud at his feet. In poor land the rice must be more closely planted, but about eight inches apart each way would be an average. The movements of an expert rice planter are so swift one can scarce follow them with the eye, yet it is at best slow work. Only an expert can plant a half acre in a day.

Before the Harvest

Once the rice is planted, if the supply of water keeps up and no flood comes to drown the rice, the farmer's duties are light till harvest approaches. Once at least—more often if low water allows weeds to grow—the children must go over the fields and pull out the weeds that grow despite the water. If any of the rice dies, fresh shoots must be set. Occasionally, if a flood kills all the rice in a limited area, the farmer can get enough young rice to replant the whole, but when planted late the crop is short.

Drought, flood, plant disease, caterpillars and crabs, are some of the difficulties with which the farmer must contend. In addition, constant watch must be kept against cattle, buffaloes and elephants, lest they eat and tread down the green rice. As harvest approaches vast flocks of birds gather and take toll, despite scarecrows and clappers and shouting boys.

Reaping and Threshing

A little before the grain is ripe the water is shut off and the fields are allowed to dry. Even then the barefoot reapers are often ankle deep in soft mud. Their reaping knives are like short sickles. Each stool of rice is cut separately and allowed to dry for a day before the rice is bound in small bundles. In Nan and Pre, the cut grain is stacked around a square of ground that is prepared as a threshing floor, but in Chieng Mai the grain is threshed at once. Rice has no chaff, and, since it has only to be broken from its stem, is easily threshed. In Chieng Mai an enormous shallow basket, ten feet in diameter, is carried from place to place in the field and the bundles of rice are beaten out over the edge. In Nan, heavy boards set at an angle are placed round the threshing floor and over these the rice is threshed out.

A Harvest Festival

Since the threshing in Nan waits a month or more on the convenience of the farmer, there is time to make it a festal occasion. Each farmer in turn, or a group of them that have stacked their rice around a single threshing floor, makes a "bee" and invites all the countryside to help thresh his rice. With laughter and jest, with feasting, and covert if not open love-making between the lads and lassies, the work goes merrily on. Minstrelsy, song and games of various kinds, have place after darkness falls on the busy scene, although, if it be moonlight, the sound of the threshing may often be heard far into the night. One disadvantage of this plan is the danger from thieves and elephants. Watch must be kept each night beside every threshing floor until the grain is threshed and carried away. The customs at Nan certainly make the threshing a picturesque scene and make the season less hurried, more merry and light-hearted than in Chieng Mai.

Buying Rice

When the harvest is on, every man is sure to ask of his employer a week off to "buy rice." He thinks he can buy it much cheaper in the field, and does not count the time he spends going from place to place, haggling over the price; perhaps he finally pays more than he would have had to pay in the first field he visited. As a matter of fact, save among friends, little rice is sold at once, the owner usually holding on in the hope of higher prices, the buyer looking for lower. But what of that? The pleasure of "buying rice" is the share in the joy of harvest; a vacation is worth much to him, as well as to you and to me, even if it brings in no shekels.

The Laos Seasons

From the beginning of the heavy rains about July 1, until in the middle of January when the last of the harvest is brought in, the time of the vast majority of the

Laos people is occupied with labor in the fields. The nearly six months that intervene before another crop must be planted is a time when farm labor is light, and the thrifty, active man seeks other employment. During these months little rain falls, and as the heat of the year culminates in March and April, it is not a time to grow anything, save in spots where abundant water for irrigation is to be had. Then it is that the thought and footsteps of men turn to the forests, where many thousands of them are employed during the dry season. But ere we follow them hither we will see a little of the work in the fields after harvest.

Gardens in the Dry Season

Where water for irrigation is abundant, a second crop of rice may be planted in February and harvested in June. There are also low-lying areas, wholly flooded during the rains, that produce a good crop at this season. The amount of dry-season rice planted increases each year, but over the bulk of the rice plains the water is insufficient to mature a second crop of rice. Even for other crops that require less water and a shorter season, the time available before the blistering heat of March and April dries up everything is very short. Tobacco, onions, garlic and some other vegetables are planted in the rice fields. As soon as the rice can be got out of the way or even earlier, as soon as the floods are over, the sand bars along every stream are hastily fenced in and prolific gardens of peppers, cucumbers, beans, sweet corn, okra, mustard, sweet potatoes and squashes, soon appear. It is not long until the receding waters leave most of these gardens high and dry. Shallow wells are dug in the sand, and by dint of many hours of labor each day with bucket and dipper these gardens are brought to maturity.

The Rice Pounder

The harvests once over, the morning markets are full once more. The very first of the new rice, patiently hulled in the rice pounder, is eagerly sought for. It has a delicate flavor that is lacking after harvest. All through the year the work of "pounding the rice" is a daily task for the women and children in every household. However, the amount of rice sold pounded, that is ready to cook, increases each year. Many families prefer to store their extra rice and pound it before selling it. Not only do they get a little higher price for it, but they have less weight to carry to market, and the bran fed to the pigs adds to the family income. Pigs are not usually allowed to run at large, but are fed by hand, not only with this bran but with weeds gathered by the children and cooked with the bran by the grandmother in a big earthen pot reserved for that purpose. The rice pounder is a big wooden mortar sunk in the ground, whose pestle is lifted by a lever with the foot and allowed to drop by its own weight. In the hands of a skilled woman it breaks less of the rice than the rice mills, but it is slow.

Other Dry-Season Employments

Having stored the harvested rice in the rice house, helped in the planting of his garden and paid his taxes, the husband and father is free to accept such remunerative employment as may come to him. The care of the garden and pigs, the watching of the buffaloes and cattle, the marketing of the surplus rice and the produce of gardens and fruit trees, can safely be left to the oversight of the wife. The dry season is therefore the time of the year when lumber is sawed, new granaries and houses and temples erected, new fields cleared, and new irrigation ditches made. In short, the thousand and one things that await a convenient season are done at that time.

Work in the Forests

Many of those employed the year round by timber companies are Kah Mooh, men of a "hill tribe," in French Laos who are particularly skilled with the ax and with elephants. They come over, a hundred together, for a few years and then return to their homes on the French side of the border. They are willing to work the entire year, and can be had more cheaply than Laos workers, and they cut most of the timber. But during the dry season a large number of Laos men are also employed to girdle the trees, to clear underbrush, and guard both standing timber and logs against fire, and to make roads for the elephants to drag the logs down the mountains. Many others are employed in cutting timber other than teak, for house posts, for lumber and for fuel, and in gathering rattan and various resins and gums used in making dammer, varnishes and lacquer.

The Drive Log Jams

Again in the months that intervene between rice-planting and harvest, September and October, especially, when the floods lift the heavy logs, many men are employed to help the elephants in the drive, working the logs off the sand bars and keeping them moving, preventing them, if possible, from gathering in a jam that closes the channel. Despite all care, some teak log will get caught and others gradually pile against it, till hundreds, even thousands of logs are piled in seemingly inextricable confusion clear across the channel. Such a jam of logs has many times endangered the bridge at Chieng Mai, and in the rapids boats sometimes must wait for days till the water goes down sufficiently for the elephants and men to be able to get at the logs, or till a higher rise sweeps all before it and clears the channel.

Elephants at Work

I know of no more interesting sight than to watch a company of elephants at work to break such a jam, and open the channel. A mahout sits on the head of each elephant to direct it, but often the intelligent animals seem themselves to know what to do. The males work with tusk, trunk and head, the females helping with trace chains attached to broad trace bands over their shoulders. One by one the key logs are pulled out, and as the mass of logs begins to move the warning "trumpet" of some watchful tusker gives the alarm, and the great beasts rush for safety to the bank or down stream. Not infrequently, one of them is injured, or even killed in the work, but still without these giants of the forest it would be difficult to handle the timber of the tropics. There is no snow to make easy the moving of enormous loads, and as yet little machinery has been introduced that could replace them.

The Elephant of Siam

Any book on Siam that gave only a passing reference to these kings of the animal kingdom would certainly be incomplete, the more so, that the largest elephants in the world are said to be those found in the forests of Siam, especially in the Laos states. Years ago, when the timber business was smaller than now, every Laos family of means had an elephant, perhaps several of them. They were used frequently on journeys as well as to drag timber and bring in the rice from the fields. It was easy then to hire them for a journey across country. The writer traveled with and on them a few times years ago. In those days they were well called the "ships of the forest." To-day the increase in the timber business has so increased the demand and enhanced the price that they are used little in other work. Only here and there can one see the "family elephants," so common not many years ago. A good tusker is now worth a thousand dollars, and only the princes, of those who have constant use for them, can afford to own one. Each year the princes who claim ownership in the wild elephants in the mountains, organize hunts to bring in those untamed children of the forests and train them for the work they alone can do. In April, 1908, twenty-five of these captives, each escorted by and chained to a tame elephant, were brought together into the city of Chieng Mai. It was a great event, and several princes, each with his retainers, mounted on elephants, went out to meet them, so that a hundred elephants or more appeared in the procession. Probably at least ten of these twenty-five captives died before they could be trained to the work and life of a captive, but the balance would bring five to ten thousand dollars to their captors. This seems cruel, but it is probably unavoidable. Nowadays there is little or no cruelty in the method of capture of the elephants, and great care is taken with their food and training.

A Rogue Elephant

Broken for the most part while still young, and treated with reasonable kindness, the trained elephants often become very docile and much attached to their keepers, but every now and then harsh treatment or inherent bad blood makes a rogue elephant. The physician in charge of the Chieng Mai Hospital, Dr. J. W. McKean, tells the following incident:

"Not long ago my friend, Dr. W. A. Briggs of Chieng Rai (to whom this book owes its best photographs) was in Chieng Mai on mission business. I asked the Chow Raja Wong, the prince who ranks next to the governor, to place some of his elephants at our disposal for photographic purposes. To this the prince readily assented. We found the palace yard well filled with elephants.

"Two particularly fine ones, the prince's favorites, were to be photographed first. To add a flavor of novelty, I suggested that His Excellency ride on the neck of the larger. He consented and proposed that I ride on the other. In a few minutes the prince, re-dressed as a mahout, mounted his tusker, and I mounted the elephant with a howdah. Dr. Briggs made one exposure, the one shown in the picture, and asked us to change position a bit before he pressed the button again. We did so; without warning the prince's beast charged mine from behind and drove him headforemost against an eight-foot solid board fence, which can be seen in the photograph behind the larger elephant. He withdrew for a moment, giving me time to spring to the fence and escape to the ground on the other side; then, thrusting his tusks into the side of my elephant just behind the fore leg, he drove him broadside through that high fence as though it had been made of straw, and pinned him up against a building beyond. Although his servants and friends were white with terror, the prince sat on the neck of that ferocious brute like the prince that he is, till the elephant's own driver, climbing to the top of the fence, sprang to the monster's back, crawled past the prince and seated himself on his head. No sooner did the brute feel his master in command, than he drew back and allowed the poor, wounded elephant to arise. The latter, although seriously injured, ultimately recovered. In terror and confusion, the other elephants had stampeded, and there were no more photographs that day. I have not sat on an elephant's neck since."

This favorite of the prince has several times tried to kill his mahout, or seriously injure other elephants, but the prince still uses and loves him.

CHAPTER VII

THE FACE OF THE LAND

Fair Laos As the mountains are round about Jerusalem, so are they round about all the Laos valleys. As the heart of the Jewish captive longed for his native hills, so the heart of the Laos man or woman out of sight of these mountains longs for the verdure-clad slopes. Even upon the foreigner who has been resident there, the charms of "Fair Laos" have laid their spell. When back in his native land, he lifts his eyes, but sees not the encircling hills to which his spirit turns. As in Japan, three fourths of the area never can be cultivated. Were the rainfall as abundant as in Japan, a larger area would be available, but rains are irregular and uncertain. Only the land that is most fertile, and most favorably situated, can profitably be cultivated, practically only that which can be irrigated.

Populous Plains. Though the Laos states as a whole are sparsely populated, some of these fertile areas have a very dense population. Stand with me on a rice plain near the center of population of the province of Lampoon, just south of the new chapel in Bahn Pan. The rice plain about you is as level as a floor, but in every direction you can see mountains that surround the great Chieng Mai plain rising to a height of four to eight thousand feet. East of you and near at hand, is the village of Muang Chee with four thousand people; to the south lies the village of Sun Ka Noi, only a little smaller; west and north are two other large villages, and within three miles of the point where we stand are a dozen other villages with one to five hundred people each. Altogether, within that radius of three miles, is a farming population of hardly less than twelve thousand people, or nearly five hundred to the square mile. Some of them may work land outside this area, but most of them depend for their support on the area in which they live. Within these limits, the population is as dense as in Belgium, only a little less dense than on the plains of China.

The Mountains Between

But only five miles away, one enters a district of forest and mountain where the traveler proceeds for three days before reaching any considerable village. There are fertile valleys to be sure, but they are narrow and isolated. Although clad with vegetation, often to their summits, the mountains are for the most part too barren or too steep for cultivation.

Nature's Own Gardens

Only in well-watered ravines and valleys among the mountains does one find that wild luxuriance of vegetation that we are apt to imagine characterizes the tropics everywhere. In such spots tree ferns, wild palms and bananas grow luxuriantly, a wealth of smaller ferns lift their graceful fronds from the crevices of the rocks, long palmlike vines of the prickly rattan are festooned from the trees. Above and around them all, more graceful than either, the clumps of bamboo curve upward and outward. One never tires of watching the ever-changing beauty of these, Nature's own gardens, especially if through the swaying foliage he catches glimpses of verdure-clad cliffs and trickling waters. Such spots of beauty may be found near the "Gates of the Mountains," in Lakawn, in the "Valley of the Four Thousand," in Nan, in "Wild Palm Glen," on the slopes of Ogre Mountain, north of Chieng Mai.

Tropical Flowers

The delicate spring flowers that are the charm of the American forest are hardly matched in the tropics. The so-called "ground orchids," that abound on the mountains in April, are nearest to them. The real orchids are mainly air plants and bloom in the clefts of tall forest trees. Just at the close of the dry season, whole forests of flowering trees blaze out in gorgeous red and yellow and pink. Many of these, as well as the more modest acacias, tamarinds and "fool beans," belong to the pea family which predominates among the flowers of Siam. Earlier in the season, thickets of certain compositæ make great masses of purple, of dull red, and of yellow, beside the path. However, flowers are sought by the Laos maidens, not for their color, but for their fragrance. The "jewel-tree" furnishes its delicate greenish flowers for their wreaths almost throughout the year. Tuberoses, golden acacias, jasmine and roses, are among the favorites. The young man is more apt to choose flowers of brilliant color, and places over his ear a sprig of "peacock-flower," or a brilliant-hued orchid.

Bird Life These brilliant flowers remind one of the plumage of the chattering little parrots that sometimes appear in almost countless numbers. Other birds of brilliant plumage flash in and out of the forest glades. White and gray cranes, pelicans and sandpipers, abound along the rivers. The myna bird perches gravely on the back of the grazing buffalo, and searches for his food, to the evident relief of the great beast. Doves not unlike our wood pigeon utter a similar note in the forest, and flocks of crows annoy the farmers as they do here. But there is a notable absence of song birds; the woods there are never vocal with their tuneful notes.

The Home of the Teak After all, it is not these garden spots of the mountains that dwell most in the memory. The rocky and somewhat barren heights are the home of the teak, most valuable of the timber trees of Siam, the greatest source of the country's wealth. The conservation and wise use of these forests has in recent years demanded and received the best thought of the government and its advisers.

Other Forest Trees

Many other trees valuable for timber, and more attractive to the eye than the teak, are also found in these mountains. Much of this timber is so dense and heavy that it will not float even when well seasoned, and it is very difficult to handle. The largest and finest of these trees are often left behind when timber is cut, because they cannot handle them. I remember especially, one giant of the forest. Nearly twelve feet in diameter at the base, its shaft towering skyward straight as an arrow, a full hundred feet, its spreading top raised still higher, it was a landmark in every direction.

God's First Temples

Among the mountains of Nan is a grove of "poo-ie" trees of little value for timber but of great beauty, that stretches along the crest of a narrow ridge for miles. Their corrugated trunks like fluted columns, and the grateful shade of their tops far, far above one's head, remind one of some Gothic cathedral or of the massive monoliths of a Grecian temple. Other trees love rather the moister soil of the river bottoms. Of these, the cotton tree which furnishes the filling for the mattresses of the country, and the oil tree which supplies a sap not unlike turpentine and a valuable timber, are both common and beautiful. The oil tree especially forms beautiful groves along the main road. Such a grove along the way from Chieng Mai to Lampoon is shown in the accompanying illustration. Notice how the towering height of the trees dwarfs the horse and

On the Road from Chieng Mai to Lampoon
A grove of oil trees

cart in the middle of the picture. Logs eighty feet in length, eight feet in diameter, and perfectly straight, have been cut in this grove.

The Sacred Po Tree

A very different tree, but not less beautiful, is seen in all the temple grounds. Under one of these "po" trees, not unlike the banyan tree, Sakya Muni, the founder of Buddhism, sat in meditation for three years ere he entered upon "the noble paths," as the principles of Buddhism are often called. In later years, he often taught under its shade, and ever since his followers have held it sacred. A large one near the writer's home was broken down in a storm, and obstructed the road. Its "sacred" wood is of no use for building, and no one dared to use it for ordinary fuel. At last the head priest decided it could be used to burn brick for a new temple, and the broken tree was thus at length cleared away. I know of few finer examples of the noble tree than the one pictured in the frontispiece. Probably a congregation of a thousand people could be seated under the shade of its spreading branches.

Denizens of the Forest

Of larger game, there is much variety in the forests of Siam. Hundreds of elephants are still found in a wild state, and carefully protected as one of the assets of the princes. The rhinoceros, too, is occasionally found. The wild ox, believed to be the progenitor of domestic cattle, is still found in the remote forests of the Laos states, and he is a magnificent beast. Quite as large and much more common, is an enormous deer with antlers not unlike those of a stag. The native name for it is "quang." The only other deer we often see is the tiny "barking deer." Bears are fairly common, and leopards often make sad havoc among young cattle, buffaloes and pigs. But it is the Bengal tiger that is most generally and most justly feared. As a rule, he does not attack man, but once he has tasted human flesh he seems satisfied with nothing else.

A Man-Eating Tiger On their return from annual meeting in Lakawn, a company of Chieng Mai missionaries camped in a rather lonely spot beside a stream. Nothing disturbed their rest, perhaps because a fire was kept up all night. Only a few nights later, a man was dragged from beside the fire at that very place, and carried off by an enormous tiger. From that time on, for months, that whole district was kept in terror by recurring instances of this tiger's boldness. Not less than twenty persons are said to have been killed, besides many cattle and pigs, by this ferocious beast. Hunts were organized, and traps set, but he always eluded his pursuers. Whether eventually he was killed, or simply left the district, no one knows, but after a time his appearances ceased. The writer has several times seen a tiger's footprints on his travels, but never has seen or heard the monster himself, although several very large tigers have been shot in the district through which he travels.

BUFFALOES ON A SAND BAR

Apes and Monkeys

Last but not least of the characteristic wild animals of "the Land of the Free," we must mention the apes and monkeys whose peculiar, reëchoing cries may often be heard among the mountains by day as well as by night. They seldom travel on the ground, but swing from tree top to tree top with a boldness that does not grow less marvelous as you watch it. Very large apes are sometimes kept as pets, and smaller ones, both black and white, are favorites of the children. In southern Siam, the long-tailed monkeys are very common in the jungles. Their grimaces and frolics are a constant amusement as one's boat creeps quietly along the narrow canals. They are also rather common in the north, but I have seldom seen them kept as pets.

The Buffalo

The domestic animals of Siam are much the same as in the United States. Horses and cattle, dogs and cats, chickens and Guinea fowl, pigs and goats, ducks, geese and turkeys—all are seen. But the most important of all their domestic animals is one never seen in America, the caribou or water buffalo. Although he is a close relative to the domestic cattle, he reminds one of a gigantic pig, and often carries a hundredweight of earth that has stuck to him from his last mud bath. He is an ungainly beast, usually very slow in his movements, but when roused or angry his speed and his enormous horns make him dangerous. However, the care of this formidable and ugly beast is usually committed to some small boy or girl, who sits the whole day long on his broad back to keep him out of the unfenced fields of growing rice. The child mounts from behind. Grasping the buffalo's tail, he steps on the projecting joint of the hind leg, and with a spring and a scramble is soon seated, with perhaps two or three others, on the monster's broad back. Strange to say, these children are seldom seriously hurt by the buffaloes, and the ungainly creature is curiously amenable to the will of his tiny keeper. The buffalo's main duty is to pull the plow and harrow morning and evening for a couple of months in the year, but the animals are also used to some extent at other seasons in hauling logs and firewood. They are never killed for food, but when they die of disease, too often the owner makes good his loss by selling the tainted meat. Many people, though they know the danger, eat it because it is cheaper than slaughtered meat.

The photograph has caught extremely well the timid, half-wild expression of these dangerous denizens of Asia, as they are startled from their noonday rest on a sand bar of the Me Yom.

CHAPTER VIII

TRADE AND TRAVEL

The Main Trade Routes

There are three main lines of travel across the Laos states: overland from Yunnan Province, China; overland to Maulmein in Burma; and up and down the river to Bangkok. Less important caravan routes radiate in every direction, reaching the remotest Laos valleys and their neighbors. Even when roads were beset by robbers, and neither life nor goods was secure, still trade along the main routes was constant. There was more danger by river than by land, so river trade was less then than now. As the country has become more settled, trade has followed the easier route, and trade by caravan across the mountains to Burma has relatively decreased.

The Haw Caravans

Every year, soon after the heavy rains are over, "English" walnuts are found in all the markets, sure sign that the "Haw" (or Yunnan Chinese) caravans of pack horses have begun to arrive. Not everyone is aware that China is the original home of these nuts. The Laos are very fond of them and so traders fill all vacant spaces in their packs. Their real loads consist of brass ware, felt blankets and furs, and sometimes opium. Also they usually bring horses and mules for sale. Although in recent years some horses have been bred in Siam, the best horses are still, as in the past, brought from China.

The Road to Burma

Most of the "Haw" caravans, after trading along from city to city, go on to Burma, and bring back loads of European piece goods, hardware and provisions, bought in Maulmein. Some of these foreign goods they carry back with them to the north, but usually they sell them in the Laos markets, and load up with Laos cotton and tobacco for the long journey back to Tali-Fu. The trip from Tali to Maulmein, via Chieng Mai and return could be made in six months, but trading along the way as the merchants do, probably eight to ten months are consumed in each round trip. Laos traders seldom go to Yunnan, but toward Burma Laos caravans share the road with the "Haws." A considerable number of cattle are driven over for sale, and their price is brought back in foreign goods, carried either by bullocks or porters, for the Laos as a rule do not use pack mules or pack horses.

Trade with Bangkok

With Bangkok, the trading is partly by river, partly overland. Boats of some size can be used on the lower river, but it is difficult and expensive to bring even the Laos boats up the rapids. Much of the coarser goods are therefore unloaded at Muang Teun, the point below the rapids nearest to Chieng Mai, and packed by bullocks over the mountains. Hundreds of tons of salt are thus carried by bullocks that go back and forth all through the dry season. Salt is seldom brought by boat direct to Chieng Mai, partly because a boat loaded with salt is hard to manage in the rapids, and a slight leak soon destroys the salt. Dry fish and some other bulky commodities are brought in the same way. For the trip southward, these bullock trains often go empty, as the bulk of freight in that direction is far less. Sometimes they carry hides, tobacco or lacquer ware; more often their baskets are filled with "meeung," wild tea leaves from the Laos hills that have been steamed and packed in bamboo joints, much as ensilage is packed in a silo. The Chinese and Siamese, as well as the Laos, chew "meeung" and derive from it much the same gentle stimulation as from tea.

Bullock Trains

Very early in the morning, one may hear the musical tinkle of the bells, as the long trains of bullocks patiently plod up hill and down, through forest and stream, twenty days' journey from Muang Teun to Chieng Mai. Before nine A. M. they have finished their day's journey. The packs are lifted from their backs, and the cattle are allowed to feed through the heat of the day. Each bullock knows his own load, and before darkness gathers, finds his way back to his place. As darkness deepens, the camp fires, lighted at the end of each row of baskets to keep off wild beasts, gleam picturesquely against the dark background of forest. All is arranged and moved with the regularity of an army encampment.

Cross-Country Trade Not only on this, but on all routes, these picturesque bullock trains are met. One year when the rice crop in Lakawn was scanty, I met dozens of them, those going east loaded with rice, those bound west hurrying back for a fresh load of the "staff of life." Two such trains collided in a narrow defile, and much confusion with endless shouting ensued ere the train could start once more. One bullock, more frisky than his neighbors, was so delighted to get safe out of the confusion, that he jumped to the path on the next ridge and rolled over and over, baskets and all, a hundred feet down till he struck a big tree. This set him free from his baskets and he jumped up none the worse for his adventure.

Humors of Trade The overland trade from province to province varies with the season, the crops and the circumstances. In a single day I met not less than thirty men, each carrying in baskets from four to ten little pigs. Evidently the crop of pigs had been short in Lakawn, or unusually abundant in Lampoon, and there was a profit of fifty cents each, enough to pay for the journey. In March, on any road leading out of Pre, there are many men loaded with Pre cotton and Pre tobacco, both of which find a market in all the other provinces, and even up in China. About the same time of year men come considerable distances to purchase brown sugar from the Me Aouw district of Chieng Mai, or palm sugar from the Me Tah valley. Just before the season for plowing begins, men carrying plowshares go out into the country. They come back loaded with leeks or peppers.

Sales are usually for cash, but every trader wants a profit both ways on his journey, so he invests his proceeds in something he can sell in his home district. Gongs for the temples and bells for cattle, elephants and horses, are brought from Burma, brass ware from China, iron from Muang Long, saltpeter for powder from the caves in Ogre Mountain.

All through the season when the roads are good and farm work light, multitudes of men yield to the "wanderlust" that is a marked feature of Laos life, and seek profit as well as pleasure in a trading expedition. Although maps are practically unknown to the common people, men can talk intelligently about the roads in every direction from their homes, often for hundreds of miles.

Although many thus journey to Burma or China, few settle there; the longing for his own village, no less strong than a desire to see the world, draws the Laos man back to his native hills.

Down the River by Boat

It remains to speak of the boat trade up and down the river. The rapids that render the Me Yom wholly unnavigable, are a serious obstacle to navigation in all the branches of the Me Nam. This boat traffic is largest on the Me Ping, the western branch of the Me Nam on which Chieng Mai is situated, but even there, no boat captain would venture down the river with a full load. Each stage of water, high or low, has its peculiar difficulties and perils, and the heavier the load the more serious these dangers become. Cocoanuts are carried down and marketed in the lower river. Boat loads of hides are often seen, and almost every boat carries "meeung," the steamed wild tea already spoken of, which is used in lieu of small coin to purchase supplies along the river. Lacquer ware, stick-lac and other gums from the forests are also carried down, but heavy commodities are rarely seen in Laos trading boats on the down-river trip.

The Up-River Trip

On the return, the boats come loaded to the gunwales with a wide variety of European goods, with salt fish from the sea and lower river, with Chinese bowls and Japanese matches, with American cotton and kerosene oil, with English prints and blankets, with India muslins and German cutlery, with bicycles and sewing machines. Even carriages and automobiles are sometimes brought.

And whence comes the money to pay for these goods? Largely from the rafts of teak logs that fill the lower river, and load hundreds of vessels each year for Europe. Teak is the only wood so far discovered that is absolutely impervious to water. Wash down a teak deck with fresh water or salt, by hand or by the dash of the waves, and

The Prince and His Elephants

the moment it is drained, it is dry. For decks, no real substitute for teak has been found; and the increasing demand for it for main and promenade decks of ocean liners constantly enhances its price in the world's markets. Her forests are the main wealth of Siam and especially of the Laos states.

How Foreigners Travel

Foreigners who have been residents in the Laos states always meet the question, "How do you travel?" The answer may vary as much as the tastes and circumstances of the individual. We travel by all the conveyances that have been mentioned; by boat, by elephant, by horse, in a sedan chair, on foot; our effects are carried by boat, by pack horses, pack mules or bullocks, by elephants, or most frequently of all by men who carry fifty to sixty pounds each in baskets over their shoulders. Travel by boat is well described in Mrs. Curtis' "The Laos of Northern Siam." To-day, by a railway journey of two days and an overland trip of eight to twelve days, it is possible to avoid the long up-river journey that usually occupies thirty to fifty days. Still, until the railway is completed to Chieng Mai, all freight and many travelers will continue to take the slower route. Even when the railway comes, the wonderful scenery of the rapids and gorge of the Me Ping will still attract the traveler.

The Ship of the Forest

I shall never forget my first journey in Laos on an elephant. It was my first experience with these "ships of the forest." With surprise, I saw them unhesitatingly climb rocks and plunge down step river banks that no other beast of burden could even attempt. Their care and sure-footedness soon took away any fear of accident. In the comfortable howdah, one may lie down at full length, or sit and read or even write, if he will but accommodate himself to the slow swing of the elephant's tread. However, after the novelty wears off, most travellers prefer to ride a pony, for a good walker will easily keep ahead of a company of elephants. The young bamboo is a favorite food of these great beasts, and it is amusing to see your monster break off a stem some inches in diameter and a dozen feet in length, and contentedly munch it as he marches along, as a child would a stick of candy. In passing through the forests, a supply of the elephant's natural food, bamboo, coarse grass, banana stalk and palm leaves is usually at hand. Their forefeet hobbled together with a chain, they seldom wander far from camp, but if frightened or drawn on in search of food, or by wild elephants in the neighborhood, they may travel long distances in the night, and lead their keepers a weary chase while the traveler waits for their return. If a baby elephant be in the company, he is sure to have much to amuse, sometimes to annoy you.

The Ponies of Siam

Few horses are raised in Siam, and they seem to degenerate in that hot climate, but a supply of ponies is brought down from China each year.

Varying in size from a Shetland pony to a polo pony, they are seldom over thirteen hands in height, but they are wiry, active little beasts with their full share of deviltry. Year in and year out they are our most common and most reliable means of transport. Even when rains swell the streams, they will patiently swim behind the ferryboat, ready when it reaches land to carry us on to the next river. Some travelers also use pack horses or pack mules to carry their food, bedding and other impedimenta. Occasionally, when there is much freight it is carried at so much a hundred by cattle or elephants, but the ordinary dependence is upon men as carriers. They can always be had on short notice. They can go in many places where the track is impracticable for pack animals, and for the missionary there is the added advanage that, when a company of carriers continues with him for weeks, he has a peculiar opportunity to influence their hearts and lives for Christ. Many of our Christian men received their first impressions of the truth, as they helped carry the "kit" of some missionary on his evangelistic tours.

CHAPTER IX

GOVERNMENT PAST AND PRESENT AMONG THE LAOS

"Dacoity"

Until 1886 when the British were compelled by Burmese misrule to take upper Burma, "dacoity," or robbery by bands of cutthroats, was common in Burmese territory. In other words, no small part of the Burmans lived by plundering their more peaceable neighbors. Even earlier than this, the firm hand of British rule had gradually narrowed the limits of these bandits, but only when Mandalay fell was it possible to suppress dacoity entirely. Forty or fifty years ago, seldom a year passed when some company of bandits did not gather among the almost inaccessible mountains along the eastern border of Burma, swoop down on some unsuspecting Laos valley, drive off the cattle, carry off men and women to a life of slavery, burn the villages, and carry terror to an area far wider than the actual scene of their depredations.

The Laos in Arms

Although the Laos are a peaceable agricultural people, when once aroused they are no mean antagonists. In recent years, a Laos constabulary, organized and drilled by foreign officers, has shown itself admirable in discipline and in other soldierly qualities, and has done much to render life and property secure in the Laos states of Siam. In the past as well, given time to rally and oppose their enemies, the Laos villagers often defeated them and drove them back. A narrow glen—one of the wildest and most beautiful I have ever seen—that leads up to a pass in the mountains west of the city of Nan is known as "Hooie See Pun," the "Ravine of the Four Thousand." The story goes that four thousand Burmans, on plunder bent, were met and annihilated in this defile by the men of Nan.

Results of Dacoity

In such raids as these, whole villages were wiped out, entire valleys depopulated, for not only were many killed by the robbers or carried off as slaves, but the survivors fled to the forests and dared not return. There, jungle fever, dysentery and other diseases, due to exposure, carried off children and adults by the score. Often the stock of rice was burned, and, since the cattle were driven off or killed, the survivors could not work their fields. Famine followed in the wake of war. A hundred and forty years ago, a Burmese army plundered and burned the cities of Chieng Mai and Lampoon, and for fifty years after that raid that whole plain, the largest and richest in the Laos states, was almost depopulated. A later raid, this time by the Siamese, destroyed Chieng Rai, and the old Laos capital, Chieng Saan. Chieng Saan has never been rebuilt, and Chieng Rai is only now recovering.

Counter Raids The Laos tribes and princes retaliated when they could. A successful raid to the north and west headed by the king of Chieng Mai brought many captives back to help repopulate the Chieng Mai Lampoon plain. Half the people of Lampoon province to-day are descendants of these subjects of the King of Burma who were thus brought down from the region of Keng Tung. Kun and Yawng, they are called, but they are Laos all, differing only very slightly in speech, in customs, or in dress, from the other people of the plain.

Slavery The forced immigrants of whom I have just spoken were not held as slaves, though slavery has always been common throughout Indo-China. The lot of a slave has not usually been a hard one, for he was usually given a home he could call his own and time to cultivate a piece of land. Sometimes, for months together, his lord would not "call" him; again his time might be wholly occupied in the service of his master. In the latter case, the slave usually received some slight money compensation, or its equivalent in a present. Three kinds of slaves have been recognized by law: hereditary slaves, slaves taken in war and debt slaves. Debt slaves have always been able to redeem themselves, though the process was made so difficult that few succeeded in doing so until a generation ago. Increasing prosperity, the influence of foreigners who have often paid redemption money and allowed the debtor to work it out, together with some change in the laws, have steadily improved conditions. A number of years ago, the enlightened King of Siam declared that all children born of slave parents after that date should be free, but this provision has never been fully enforced in the Laos states. The "chow," or native princes, are the principal slave-holders and, naturally, since they are the judges, every obstacle has been placed in the way of emancipation. Still, as Siamese rule has become more direct in the north, slavery is fast disappearing.

Unjust Exactions

Forty years ago misgovernment at home made worse the insecurity of life and property due to robber raids. At that time, and to a less extent even ten years ago, it was unwise for a Laos "man of the people" to betray in any way the possession of property. If he built a better house, or a new rice bin, if he acquired more cattle than were necessary to work his bit of rice plain, only a generous bribe to the petty prince, or "chow," on whom he was dependent, could save him from ruinous taxation or a forced loan. If his bananas or vegetables were better than those of his neighbors, a minion of the "chow" was almost sure to stop his wife or daughter on the way to market, and relieve her of the best of the contents of her baskets. For produce thus taken, payment was seldom made, and there was no redress. His person was hardly more safe than his property.

Are the Laos Lazy? The Laos are often called lazy, unjustly, I think. No man who is not compelled to do so, works regularly if he does not expect to receive the fruit of his labor. When the conditions I have just described were prevalent, what possible motive was there for industry or thrift? Conditions have changed, but the habits of a lifetime are difficult to change. The older men are still indolent, but a spirit of industry and thrift has grown greatly among the younger men in the past fifteen years. Now well-built frame houses with tile roofs are to be found in almost every village, better vegetables and fruits are in the markets, a better quality of foreign goods is demanded; the whole country is more prosperous. These advances have been brought about largely by the change in governmental conditions noted in the next paragraphs.

The Old Régime Up to 1828 the Laos princes ruled their own people. At various times they paid tribute, or sent presents, to Burma, to Cambodia, to Pegu, to the Kings of Siam; not infrequently to two or more of them at the same time. One district and its people, now ruled by Great Britain, derives its name, "Sam Tow" (or "Three Allegiances") from the fact that it sent tribute more or less regularly to Burma, to China and to Siam. These various claims of their neighbors had never been effectively or continuously enforced. The princes themselves probably looked on the gifts sent merely as a sort of insurance. Had a real leader arisen, he might have built up a permanent and independent Laos empire, but whether in war or in peace, the Laos have never long been united. At different times, the King of Chieng Saan, of Lampoon, of Sawankaloke, of Bassak or of Wieng Chan, has been recognized as "King of the Laos," but usually for only a short time consecutively.

About one hundred years ago, the King of Wieng Chan, a city on the Cambodia River, some three hundred miles northeast of Bangkok, was regarded by the Siamese, justly, perhaps, as the King of all the Laos. He had at times given tribute or presents to the King of Siam. Later he refused it. The result was a war, in 1828, in which the city of Wieng Chan was destroyed and its inhabitants carried off in a body as war captives. The descendants of these captives are still held as the slaves of Siam, attached to the royal palace and temples in Pechaburee. (How the edicts of emancipation have affected them, I do not know.)

Origin of Siamese Rule

The Siamese seem to have claimed that the capture of Wieng Chan gave them authority over all the Laos. Whether their claim be based on that, or on previous conditions, matters little: the fact is that most of the Laos states have pretty regularly acknowledged some measure of subjection to Siam ever since. At first, little more than the right of investiture with golden betel box and other insignia of authority, and stated visits of ceremony to Bangkok with certain formal presents, was required of the princes in the north. Even these shadowy signs of subjection were never regularly enforced east and north of the Cambodia River, or north of Chieng Saan. Still the King of Siam at times claimed sovereignty all the way to the borders of China.

Drawing the Lines Closer

Over the nearer Laos states, Siamese authority was gradually more effectively enforced. Twenty years ago, the power of life and death had already been taken from the Laos princes, and a Siamese official, known to English residents as the Siamese commissioner, was located at the capital of each province. Nominally merely the adviser of the Laos ruler, these commissioners gradually drew closer the bonds that united the Laos states to the kingdom of Siam. In 1895, when the writer first went to Nan, the authority of the Siamese commissioner in that province was still rather shadowy, though even then orders from Bangkok were rapidly becoming the real power in Chieng Mai and Lakawn. Opposition to Siamese authority and methods was the real cause of the so-called "Shan Rebellion" in 1902, but the suppression of that uprising was the occasion for measures that have made Siamese rule effective in every hamlet within the boundaries of the kingdom.

Difficulties of the Siamese

Doubtless the Laos people are to-day more or less restive under Siamese rule. However good their intentions, Siamese officials are dealing with a people who look on them as foreigners, and who do not appreciate that many of the acts of these foreigners are for their own real advantage. For instance, when roads are planned, they are made by men who see only the hardship of enforced unpaid labor, often far from home, and at a season when their own interests suffer by their absence. Moreover, owing to the lack of intelligent administrators, few enough under any government, rules for the direction of these workmen must sometimes be enforced to the letter, if they are to be enforced at all. A rule good in the main often involves unnecessary labor and hardship where an administrator with discretion as to details could modify it to advantage. Only as we realize the difficulties under which it labors, can we appreciate the real results of Siamese rule. What have some of these results been?

Beneficent Results of Siamese Rule

First. Life and property in the Laos states are more secure than under the rule of the native princes. Police regulations are better and better enforced. The Laos constabulary or gendarmerie, trained under Danish officers, is an increasingly efficient body of men. Enforcement of a uniform law, instead of the different laws of several states, has in itself brought better order. The Siamese law is not in all respects an improvement; especially as regards marriage and the family, the old Laos customs were better. We may hope that the recently enacted criminal code, which seeks to adapt to the East the best in the laws of the West, may prove better than either.

The new courts, too, are far better than the old. Far from perfect, of course, they are good in principle and fairly well administered. On the whole, then, life and property are more secure than under the old régime.

Second. The country is more prosperous. Taxes and exactions, especially enforced labor, may at times bear hard on the people. Public improvements may have been pushed faster than was wise, involving serious hardship to many. Pay promised for labor has in some cases not been forthcoming. The fact remains that taxes are more uniform, more certain and more just, than under the rule of the princes. Prosperity and a sense of security are shown in the better houses that are everywhere being built. Better methods of agriculture, better facilities for transport and trade, have come with new roads.

Third. Good beginnings have been made in public education, in the suppression of slavery and gambling, in systems of account and record, in all that constitutes the outward forms of modern civilization. The king and his advisers have made mistakes, but the fact remains that His Majesty the King of Siam is justly spoken of as one of the most progressive and wisest statesmen in Asia; that the changes quietly introduced and effectively carried out by the Siamese in the north during the last twenty years are a marvel to one who has seen both the old régime and the new.

Sixty-five Descendants of Noi Soonya, one of the two Martyrs
Dr. McGilvary in center. All are Christians

CHAPTER X

THE COMING OF THE GOSPEL

The Pioneers

On June 20, 1858, two young Americans landed together at the port of Bangkok, Siam, who were destined to continue for more than fifty years in that far-away tropical land associations begun in student days in Princeton. They were Rev. Daniel McGilvary and Rev. Jonathan Wilson, both of whom, after fifty-one years of service in the Land of the White Elephant, are still (1909) actively engaged in the work they love. Ere we trace the later history, let us consider for a moment the conditions of missionary work in Siam when they reached Bangkok in 1858.

Beginnings of Mission Work in Siam

While the gates of China were still closed to missionary effort, both the Baptist and the American boards sent missionaries to work among the Chinese residents of Bangkok. The Baptists have in a measure continued this work among the Chinese, and have to-day several Chinese and Peguan-speaking churches in and near Bangkok. However, when the doors of China were opened, most of these workers were transferred to that empire. In 1818, Mrs. Ann Hazeltine Judson set herself to acquire the Siamese language and translated a catechism and the Gospel of Matthew into that tongue. It was printed at Serampore the following year, but for a long time thereafter Siam was still regarded mainly as a point of approach to China.

Missions to the Siamese

The first missionaries to direct their efforts mainly to the Siamese themselves were sent by the American board. D. B. Bradley, M. D., whose long, varied and fruitful labors in Siam entitle him to be considered the father of missions there, reached Bangkok in 1835, and continued in the work until his death in 1873. At that time (1835), the American board drew its support and its missionaries from Presbyterian as well as Congregational churches, and later, when the fields of labor were divided, responsibility for the evangelization of Siam and its people was assumed by the Presbyterian Church. Therefore, though several of the earliest and most influential of the early missionaries were Congregationalists, it is generally recognized that the Laos as well as the Siamese are peculiarly a Presbyterian field. Practically no other church is at work there.

Missons and Social Progress

Before Messrs. McGilvary and Wilson arrived in Siam, schools had been opened for both boys and girls, and medical work had helped to open the doors. Perhaps the most far-reaching result of the work had been due to the fact that Rev. Jesse Caswell was invited to act for some years as the tutor of the prince who afterwards became King of Siam. While neither he nor his son, the present progressive ruler of Siam, accepted Christianity, they always showed the utmost friendliness to the missionaries and their work, and they sought and followed their advice in the effort to bring morals and social conditions in Siam into line with the best standards the West has to offer. The abolition of slavery, vaccination, the institution of public hospitals and schools, and the abolition of public gambling, are some of the changes that are traceable in no small measure to the influence of American missionaries. As a Siamese prince expressed it, "Siam has been opened to the world, not by the guns of western nations, but by the American missionaries."

The Situation in 1858

In 1858, while very few had openly accepted Christ (in fact, the missionaries who arrived in 1858 witnessed the baptism of the first Siamese convert), influences had nevertheless been set at work that have profoundly affected the morals and policies of Siam ever since. The organized work of the mission at that time was still confined to the capital itself, and Mr. McGilvary, in association with Rev. S. G. McFarland, was privileged in 1861 to share in opening at Petchaburee, ninety miles west of Bangkok, the first outside station. He soon came in contact there with the Laos captives who, at the capture of Wieng Chan in 1828, had been brought down as war captives and attached as serfs to the royal palace and temples at Petchaburee. Becoming interested in them, his heart went out in the desire to carry the gospel to their brethren in the far-away north country. He asked and obtained permission from the mission and from the Siamese Government to visit the Laos states in 1863. He came back fully determined to follow God's leading into that distant land. Rev. Jonathan Wilson joined him in the request to the mission and to the board at home for permission to begin work in Chieng Mai, then as now, the largest city in the Laos states. The permission was granted. April 1, 1867, found Rev. Daniel McGilvary with Mrs. McGilvary and two children in Chieng Mai, and Rev. Jonathan Wilson and Mrs. Wilson joined them a year later. That first year was one of much trial and yet of great opportunity. Until more permanent quarters could be obtained, the King of Chieng Mai granted them the use of a "sala" or rest house in the market place. There, under the shade of a spreading banyan tree, surrounded by all the confusion of an eastern market place, in a building that afforded little privacy, and imperfect protection from the rays of a tropical sun, the first year was passed. Visitors were constant and seed was sown that brought forth fruit, not in Chieng Mai alone, but in distant provinces as well.

Opening of the Laos Mission

The Laos Language vs. the Siamese

Messrs. Wilson and McGilvary, having lived for nine years in lower Siam, were familiar with the Siamese language. Then, as now, the Siamese claimed suzerainty over the Laos, and there was an increasing use of the Siamese language and desire to learn it among the people. Much of the Bible had already been translated into Siamese, and missionary work was begun through the medium of that language. Indeed, for many years it was assumed that the translation of the Scriptures into the Laos language was unnecessary. But as a Christian Laos community grew up, the demand for a Laos Christian literature grew in force and urgency. Not only are the differences in vocabulary, word forms and idiom, very considerable, but the written character is wholly different. After some years, Laos type was devised, and the twenty-fifth anniversary of the opening of the mission was marked by the publication of Matthew and a catechism in the Laos character. While the use of Siamese is now rapidly increasing among the Laos people in Siam, those outside the borders of Siam—more than half of all the Laos people—know nothing of Siamese. The mission press at Chieng Mai is the only establishment in the world that can now print the Laos character, and the work it does for the government with the sale of our own literature, makes it entirely self-supporting. The day is probably far distant when the Siamese language will replace that of the Laos in our work.

How Work Began

The first missionaries did not find differences of language a serious barrier, but quickly found a way to the hearts of the kindly Laos race. Prediction of an eclipse helped to break one of the common superstitions, and led to the conversion of Nan Inta, the first Laos man to receive Christian baptism. Vaccination, the use of quinine and other simple remedies, and kindness shown to the sick, won the confidence of others. But conversation with the visitors that crowded their homes, as well as with those whom the missionaries visited in their own homes—quiet personal evangelism—was the means most used of God to bring the Laos people to Christ. Bazaar preaching, or any preaching to large crowds, has never been a prominent feature of work among the Laos. School work was soon begun for the children of those who had shown interest in the gospel, but then as now, few children from non-Christian homes were enrolled in the schools. A Christian primary school within the reach of every Christian Laos boy or girl has been our aim, and even in our higher schools few "outsiders" are enrolled, and but little effort has been put forth to make our schools a direct evangelizing agency. However, this has been due to the lack of sufficient teaching force, rather than to a distinct policy of the mission.

"Dr. McGilvary's Long Tours"

Very soon after his arrival, Dr. McGilvary began the long tours that took him within five or six years into every Laos province where organized work has since been done. Till he was past seventy years of age, his rule was to spend the dry season of each year in a tour to distant provinces, or outlying districts where the gospel had not yet been heard, or where he could reach some visitor to his home in Chieng Mai who had gone back with some knowledge of the truth. In these journeys he explored a territory larger than Indiana and Ohio combined, that had been up to that time practically unknown to the world. The writer will never forget the return of Dr. McGilvary from the last and perhaps the longest of these long tours. He had seen the vision of French Laos won for Christ as never before, but had been compelled by opposition from the government to relinquish most promising work there for the time, at the very beginning of the rains. For more than a month on the return journey he was never long dry by day, often not at night; again and again he swam his horse over the swollen streams, and it is a marvel how the Master preserved the life and health of his aged servant on that long and perilous journey. We hope that soon his own story of those pioneer days and journeys may be in the hands of the church.

Persecution and Death

Though trials and hardships had from the first been faced both by the missionaries and by the new converts, open persecution did not arise until seven converts had been baptized and many others had shown a deep interest in the gospel message. The King of Chieng Mai had favored the coming of the missionaries, and promised to his suzerain, the King of Siam, to protect them; he rather suddenly became a bitter opponent of the work. Dr. McGilvary called upon him to ask the reason of this opposition. The answer was in substance, "Go on, teaching if you will, I cannot prevent it; but just as soon as any of my people accept your religion, off go their heads." The story of that persecution will appear at length in the memoirs Dr. McGilvary will soon publish. The king did kill two of the seven Christians, and would have killed the rest had they not hidden or fled. They were "all scattered abroad except the apostles" (the missionaries), but, "they that were scattered abroad went about preaching the word," quietly and secretly, indeed, but none the less effectively. The boldness of the martyrs in the face of death and their unfaltering witness for Christ, had influenced their very executioners.

Proclamation of Religious Liberty to the Laos

Though the lives of the missionaries were for a long time in danger, and though they were urged to withdraw for the time, they still remained at their post. God's hand was laid on the persecuting king and within a year he was dead. The daughter who succeeded him was more favorable to mission work, and both she and her consort were to the end warmly friendly to the missionaries. Still a crisis came again in 1878, when two Christians whose relatives were still demon-worshipers, wished to marry without the customary offerings to the demons. An appeal was finally made to the King of Siam. His answer was the "Proclamation of Religious Liberty to the Laos," that has since been to the Laos Christians the charter of their liberties. While there have since been several cases of long imprisonment on false charges and many cases of petty persecutions, and while even to-day the lot of the new Christian is often far from easy, open persecution has ceased.

Lengthening the Cords An early—perhaps the earliest—believer among the Laos, though baptized later than some others, was San Ya We Chai, a resident in Chieng Saan, an old capital of the Laos, one hundred and fifty miles north and east of Chieng Mai. He had been a frequent visitor at the "rest house" in the market place in Chieng Mai during the first year of Dr. McGilvary's work. At that time, business had kept him temporarily in that city. By word of mouth, and through the printed Siamese Scriptures which he could read with some difficulty, he had gained some definite knowledge and conviction of the truth as it is in Jesus. On his return to his home in the north, he became the nucleus and leader of a circle of believers in the old capital. A few years later Dr. McGilvary visited him there, and organized into a Christian church the group of believers in Chieng Saan—the first church at a distance from Chieng Mai. Out of that little band have grown the six organized churches within the bounds of Chieng Rai station. Even before a missionary was resident there, the membership had become three hundred. No other part of the Laos field is showing to-day as rapid and vigorous growth as that district. This is partly due to the fact that it is rapidly filling up by immigration from more crowded districts; for released in a measure from the restraint of custom and kinship, the immigrant is peculiarly open to new truth. A part of the growth is also due to the fact that, from the first, the spirit of that church has been peculiarly self-helpful.

Strengthening the Stakes

In 1871, C. W. Vrooman, M. D., joined the band of pioneers in Chieng Mai, and definite organized medical missionary work was begun there. Although Dr. Vrooman remained but two years, he shared in at least one of Dr. McGilvary's long tours and so carried to distant provinces some knowledge of foreign medicine. Marion A. Cheek, M. D., succeeded him, and was instrumental in gathering the means for a hospital building.

The recovery from the effects of the persecution was at first slow, but eventually—as in other lands—the blood of the martyrs was the seed of the church. Some time since, seventy-three descendants, to the third and fourth generation, of Noi Soonya, one of the martyrs, were on the rolls of the churches in Chieng Mai province. It was not, however, until about 1885 that accessions to the church began to be large. The membership increased from 152 in 1884 to 1841 in 1894.

During these years, a considerable number of

native evangelists were employed by the mission, and its first and noblest native minister was ordained to the gospel ministry. Kroo Nan Ta had been for years the favorite of the king among all the Buddhist monks, and was probably the most learned among them all. Even after he became a Christian, any question of Buddhist philosophy was apt to be referred to him by his old associates. Before the persecution he had become a secret believer, and his friendship for the missionaries was so well known that he was compelled to flee. For nearly ten years he wandered to distant lands. As a monk he had practiced the sternest austerities known to Buddhist asceticism. He had gone once from Chieng Mai to Lampoon, eighteen miles, measuring his length on the ground like a measuring worm, and was accounted peculiarly holy. Still his heart could find no rest. He returned to Chieng Mai and declared himself a follower of Christ. Already a learned man and familiar with the Christian Scriptures, he soon became the right-hand man of the missionaries in evangelistic work. With tireless energy and zeal he traveled up and down the land. Welcomed in Buddhist temples and in the homes of princes as no other of our evangelists could be, he was no less welcome in the home of the lowliest, until worn out in his labor of love, he fell asleep in 1898.

Bread Cast on the Waters

In 1877, a venerable man, evidently of high rank, came to the physician in Chieng Mai asking medicine for his deafness, and referred to the cure Christ had wrought on a deaf man. He was a high official at the court in Lakawn who, twenty years before, had received Christian books from Dr. Bradley in Bangkok. He had read and pondered, and, so far as he could understand, had given inward assent to the truth, but in all those twenty years of steadfast adherence to what he understood, he had found no one to teach him. The skill of the physician was blessed to his recovery. He gave his heart to Christ and was baptized, the first fruits of Lakawn for Christ. As soon as he was known to be a Christian, he was ordered back to Lakawn. He said, "If they want to kill me because I worship Christ, I will let them pierce me." His life was spared, but office, wealth, friends and social position were taken away. Yet the aged man remained firm. His consistent stand for Christ led the missionaries to send evangelists to begin work in his province of Lakawn.

Opening of Lakawn Station

In 1885, Rev. Jonathan Wilson and Dr. and Mrs. Peoples opened there the second station of the Laos mission. Though from two to four missionary families have been at work there now for over twenty years, and promising boarding schools both for girls and for boys, as well as most successful medical missionary work, have helped to sow the seed, the work has proved harder and less immediately fruitful than in some other provinces. The poverty of the people, due to repeated crop failures and famine, has had something to do with this. Still, in proportion to their numbers and means, no church among the Laos surpasses the three hundred Christians in Lakawn church in their gifts to the work of the Lord. The new hospital and new buildings for the schools erected by the generosity of friends, have given added facilities for all departments of the work. Lakawn is the present objective point of the railway to the north, and not improbably will be made the center of government for the Laos states when it reaches there. From the standpoint of mission work, as well as business and government, Lakawn is likely to be relatively more important in the future than in the past. Moreover, it is hoped that the reconstruction of an old dam and system of ditches, destroyed many years ago in a great flood, has removed the danger of famine that has hung over the province for a generation.

Famine and a New Station

The famine of 1893 affected not only Lakawn province, but Pre as well. Considerable sums of money were sent to the missionaries to be used in the relief of suffering. Kindness thus shown opened the hearts of many in both provinces to the gospel message, and additions to the force of the mission that year made it possible to open a new station in Pre. Circumstances have interfered with the steady progress of work, and no missionary has for several years resided there, but the mission feels that work there must be pressed and expects the coming year to place missionaries once more in that inviting field.

Work in Nan Province

As early as 1872, and several times in later years, Dr. McGilvary and his associates visited the city and province of Nan. In area and population it is second only to Chieng Mai among the Laos states of Siam, possibly not to that. Its rulers have been the noblest of the Laos princes, men of dignity and ability, who retained longer than the other princes a considerable independence of Siamese authority. More conservative than other provinces, it has presented some special difficulties to the messengers of the cross. In 1895 Dr. and Mrs. Peoples, who had shared in opening the work in Lakawn, asked and gained the consent of the mission to open in Nan the fourth station. At present the church in that province reports a membership of one hundred and ninety with five out-stations. The church that supports Mrs. Peoples has recently supplemented the gifts of the native church, and erected there a memorial chapel that worthily represents the gospel to all passers by, and is more adequate to their needs than the crowded chapels in most of our stations and out-stations.

Chieng Rai and the Unoccupied Fields

In December, 1896, the mission appointed Rev. W. C. Dodd and C. H. Denman, M. D., to open the station in Chieng Rai that it had long planned for. Unlike most new stations, Chieng Rai was not a new field; it was one where the growth of the work from small beginnings had become too large and too important to be managed at long range. As Mr. Phraner once put it, it was as if the pastor of a great and growing church in San Francisco should reside in New York and be able to make to it only brief and occasional visits. The growth of the work since the opening of Chieng Rai as a station, has been steady and constant. The immigration from other provinces to repeople the districts devastated by war early in the century, has given to the workers there a population exceptionally open to the influences of the gospel. Thus in 1897 the organized work of the mission had measurably covered that part of Siam known distinctively as the Laos states. However, along the lower course of the Cambodia River is a vast area wholly Laos, but as yet wholly untouched by missionary effort. The same may be said of the Laos population of Muang Tahk or Raheng. Only half the Laos territory of Siam itself has as yet been touched in any way by our mission work.

Work in French Territory

In his earlier tours, Dr. McGilvary had several times crossed the Mekong or Cambodia River, and in 1873 had visited Luang Prabang, now the capital of French Laos. In 1893, in company with the Rev. Robert Irvin, he made a long tour to the north following the course of the Cambodia River, well into Chinese territory. In 1897, when Dr. Peoples was his travel companion, most of their time was spent in French territory. A special opening for the gospel was discovered among the Kah Mook, the hill tribe from whom the timber companies draw many of their forest workers. These people are not Laos, but most of the men understand the Laos tongue. Both Dr. McGilvary and Dr. Peoples urged upon the mission at its next meeting the call for a new station in French territory, primarily for the Kah Mook who had shown such eagerness to receive the gospel message, but also for the more numerous Laos people among whom they dwell. Permission to open a station has never been obtained from the French Government, and serious obstacles have been put in the way of any organized work there. But visits by Dr. McGilvary in 1899, Dr. Dodd in 1901, and by Messrs. Campbell and McKay in 1904, have helped to maintain the interest first aroused. This year (1909) the Laos native church voted to make that their own mission field. A hundred communicants, faithful amid many difficulties as well as many inquirers, call for the earnest prayer of the church for this orphan company of believers three hundred miles from any other Christians, whom the selfish policy of the French has forbidden the missionary to visit.

Work in British Territory

Meantime, the thought and effort of the mission and of the native church had been turned in another direction, toward Keng Tung, the center of Laos population in British territory. An exploring tour carried out in 1897 by Messrs. Dodd, Briggs and Irwin, led the mission, in December, 1898, to ask permission of the board to open a station there as well as in French territory. From that time native evangelists or missionaries, or both, have visited British territory each dry season, and in 1904 organized work was begun in Keng Tung city. The Baptists of Burma looked upon this as in some sense an invasion of their territory. Circumstances have led the board to yield to them, and withdraw the resident missionaries from that city, although we still carry on the work in the province by frequent tours from Chieng Rai.

Touring in Chinese Territory

In at least four different tours our missionaries have crossed the Chinese border and found the people friendly, accessible, and willing to listen to the gospel, but no organized or permanent work has ever been undertaken there, nor can it be, until we are ready to open a permanent station. Our missionaries in Keng Tung came constantly in contact with trading caravans, who told them that for a distance as far to the north as Raheng lay to the south (four hundred and fifty miles by road, or three hundred and fifty as the crow flies) the Laos language and character are still in use in market and monastery alike. Although a vigorous native church of four thousand communicants has been gathered in the district within reach of our mission stations, the great bulk of the Laos people, and of the territory they occupy, is still totally untouched by the gospel.

Is the Presbyterian Church in the United States of America planning for anything less than the conquest of the whole Laos people for Christ?

CHAPTER XI

TOURING AND TEACHING

The Aim of Touring

Mention has already been made of "long tours" to the north and east by Dr. McGilvary and others, that revealed how vast is the territory yet to be possessed, how wide open many of the doors. This chapter will speak rather of regular touring work within the limits of each station. I put touring and teaching together to emphasize the fact that, save in districts where no organized work has been done, the work of teaching occupies a larger share of the missionary's time than the direct proclamation of the gospel. In training the rank and file of native Christians to be missionaries to their own relatives and neighbors, he multiplies himself, and places his work on a solid basis. Missionaries may come and missionaries may go, but the native church remains. With God's help, it must live and grow, till the whole land and all its people have been won for Christ.

Beginning of an Out-Station

As the work among the Laos people has grown, the duty of maintaining regular Sabbath and evening worship in their own homes and villages has constantly been laid on the new believers.

TABLE OF DISTANCES AND TRAVEL IN THE LAOS MISSION

From	To	Miles	Time Required	Means of Travel	Remarks
Bangkok	Chieng Mai	600	6 to 8 weeks	Native boats	A series of 40 rapids prolongs the journey to Chieng Mai.
"	Lakawn	550	5 to 6 weeks	" "	Rapids render journey difficult.
"	Pre	500	3 days: 2 days. By rail, 1 day by pony.		
"	Nan	600	5 weeks	Native boats	Rapids render journey difficult.
"	Keng Tung	870	10 to 11 weeks	Boat and pony travel	The last 2 or 3 weeks of the way very mountainous.
Chieng Mai	Chieng Rai	120	8 days	Pony or Elephant	Mountainous.
"	Lampoon	18	½ "	Pony or Carriage	Good road.
"	Lakawn	65	4 "	Pony or Elephant	Mountainous.
"	Pre	120	8 "	" " "	"
"	Nan	240	15 "	" " "	"
"	Keng Tung	270	22 "	" " "	Very mountainous.
Chieng Rai	Keng Tung	150	13 "	" " "	" "
Lakawn	Chieng Rai	145	9 "	" " "	No mountains.
Nan	Chieng Rai	160	13 "	" " "	

N. B.—The Royal Siamese Railway, now being built, at present (1910) is within one day's travel of Pre. It is to be extended to Lakawn and Chieng Mai, and probably eventually to Chieng Rai.

People of several adjacent villages often unite in these services. As time passes on, perhaps very soon, their interest and efforts draw in relatives and friends. Leaders and elders are chosen, and the new center becomes a recognized out-station of the mission. Seventy-two such centers of Christian influence were reported by the mission in 1907.

The Missionary's Field and Force

Each missionary, medical as well as clerical, is made responsible for oversight of the work in one or more of these out-stations. The district about it is his peculiar field. The Christians in it are his working force. To maintain interest and attendance upon the services in distant and widely scattered villages, to secure growth in knowledge and grace, and to make of these men and women, weak and ignorant, but with the love of God in their hearts, leaven that shall leaven the whole lump, is the constant problem of the touring missionary.

While he ever seeks and finds opportunity to present the gospel to "outsiders," to those who have not yet "entered the religion of Jesus," still the best work of the missionary in districts where the gospel has already found entrance, is done through the native Christians, not independent of them. His heart is often gladdened by an invitation to visit a home where the work and words of some Laos brother or sister have already aroused interest in the gospel message.

Intension Versus Extension Multitudes of villages, some of them quite near our mission stations, are yet untouched by the gospel; whole districts, a little more distant, but easily within reach, have still no Christians. Neither these nor the wider field yet untouched, must be forgotten and neglected, but the touring missionary or evangelist usually visits first his established out-stations, seeking to "strengthen the stakes," that from them he may "lengthen the cords," to reach and hold the whole land for Christ. Two distinct phases of evangelistic effort are thus indicated, the intensive and extensive; one seeks to deepen conviction and increase knowledge in hearts and districts already touched by the gospel; the other reaches out to the regions that are beyond. Of either one it may be said, "These ought ye to have done, and not to leave the other undone."

The Touring Season Touring is done at all seasons of the year, and touring during the rains or the rice season has its own advantages as well as its peculiar difficulties. However, most of the touring work, especially that in which the ladies of the mission share, must be done between January and June. These months between rice harvest and rice-planting are often spoken of as the "touring season." The people are then less busy and more accessible than at other seasons. "Roads," if such we may call them, are then at their best, and neither mud nor floods stand in the traveler's way. Language study, literary work and other parts of a missionary's duty that can be postponed to a convenient season, fill in the months when traveling is difficult or impossible. From January to June almost all the families in the mission spend at least a part of their time in field work.

Keeping in Touch with the Field

During the touring season, the evangelists employed by the native church, as well as the missionaries themselves, are most active. The little army of self-supporting vaccinator evangelists referred to in the next chapter are then sent out. Different plans are employed in different stations to keep in touch with these native workers, and make their efforts effective. In Chieng Mai, the number of workers is larger than elsewhere, and more systematic oversight is possible. The vaccinators come in for instruction three or four days each month, and the other evangelists, whether employed by the native church or by the mission, usually come to share in the instruction and inspiration of these gatherings. As the evangelists and vaccinators represent in their persons nearly every out-station in Chieng Mai and Lampoon provinces, and go out for their work over an even wider area, the missionaries are able through them to come into intimate touch with every part of the field.

Starting Out for a Tour

At the close of each session, the missionaries as well as the native workers go out for another month of hand-to-hand work. Let us follow them into the field. In imagination we will join a party on a tour to the north from Chieng Mai.

It is a Thursday afternoon. A pack pony, a cook and several carriers, as well as two native evangelists have gone out earlier in the day, but the missionary is delayed by callers till nearly night. He rides out and overtakes his men twelve miles from the city, not as he expected in a village where there are Christians, but camped in a rest house by the roadside. It is too late for any formal services, and a little rain is falling, but after supper several of the party find opportunity to talk with other travelers and villagers, and at evening worship, despite the rain, some others are present.

On the March Bright and early the next morning the cavalcade is on the march. In several villages by the way the missionary pauses at the home of a lonely Christian family, or of an acquaintance who has shown interest in the truth. At noon he tarries two hours in a Christian village, visits some of the homes, and holds a brief service, but he cannot remain longer lest he fail to reach his appointment for the Sabbath, which is still far away. Night finds him camped beside the home of a man who knows Dr. McGilvary, and has heard something of the truth. The use of the stereopticon brings a crowd of villagers to see and hear the story of the life and love of the Saviour of men. Several remain to question further, but are not ready to commit themselves. May the seed thus sown be not in vain.

An Out-Station

An early start and a long day's journey over the mountains bring the party Saturday evening to the chapel at Muang Pao. This is one of the largest and most vigorous out-stations in Chieng Mai province, but so distant and difficult of access that it cannot be frequently visited. Just now the work there is particularly important, because there has been a large immigration from other more densely populated districts. These immigrants, separated from home ties and surroundings, are peculiarly open to new influences. Three full days there will enable the missionary and evangelists to visit most of the Christian homes. Daily classes for the children, the women and the men, and evening services for all, are held. The Sabbath is especially full, and nearly every Christian household for five miles around is represented in the services. A definite agreement is made to begin school the following week. Word comes later that nearly forty pupils are enrolled. Schools like this draw no money from the board, being supported by tuition and other contributions.

A Hard Day's Journey

From Muang Pao, a long day of hard travel up the mountains and then down the beautiful valley of Wild Palms and along a stream that loses itself in a cleft in a rock, on past Ogre Mountain with its caves, from which the country's supply of saltpeter comes, brings the party to Chieng Dao, a distant out-station that has suffered by removals and insufficient oversight. Here several days are spent in

A Laos Maid

instruction, council and encouragement, going from house to house among a widely scattered flock. Here, as everywhere, the stereopticon and picture roll aid in bringing the people together. Encouraged and strengthened by this too hurried visit, the people not only gather in unusual numbers for the Sabbath services, but subsequently show greater zeal and perseverance. On the return journey both nights are spent in villages where isolated Christian families are holding out faithfully amid difficult surroundings.

A Family on a Tour

In 1906, every missionary family in Chieng Rai spent many weeks in touring. Mr. White described their trip as follows:

"Early in February, we packed our belongings, closed the house, and spent five very happy weeks among the Christians south and west of the city. As we stopped for dinner at Me Sooie, several men doing business at the court that day called on us and urged us to visit their villages. Two said: 'Do you not remember us? You gave us tracts in a temple in Chieng Rai.' Since then it has been my privilege to receive one of those men to full communion. 'Baby Elizabeth,' 'Baby Bilhorn' (the organ) and a magic lantern were irresistible attractions, and wherever they went we had splendid audiences. The chief prince of Muang Fang invited us to his residence to show the pictures, and the immense house was packed with his friends and retainers. In Wieng Pa Pao, homes closed to us last year invited us to hold services with them. It was a glad day for Pa Pao church when these wanderers returned. At another village we found a good old deacon, whose prayers for the sick and ailing ones in the community have had most remarkable answers. Another Christian, with beaming face, invited us to come and examine seven catechumens. Poor, spirit-ridden people, chased from village to village, they had fled to the Christians at Wieng Pa Pao and been gladly received and kindly treated. Now they were eager to profess their faith in the Saviour who had delivered them from the power of the demons. We found also two men over sixty years of age (and therefore exempt) who had paid the four tical poll tax rather than take a heathen oath as to their age. Altogether this trip and the year was a most happy one."

Touring in the Wet Season

Those of our missionaries who give most time to evangelistic work are out nearly every month in the year. The following from Dr. McKean, of Chieng Mai, tells of some such work:

"The missionary has no Sabbath day of rest. No day is a harder strain on his spiritual and physical nature than the Sabbath. Last Sabbath, for instance, the missionaries in Chieng Mai spent the day as follows: Harris went to Me Dawk Deng, twelve miles distant. The rice season is here and the fields are overflowed. It is practically impossible to go with a horse at all, nor could he reach the chapel in time if he went Sabbath morning. After teaching school on Saturday, he started out on foot. Plowing through mud and water, crossing innumerable irrigating ditches, one stream up to his neck and no bridge, zigzagging across the fields on the narrow rice ridges, he finally reached his destination, and after a night's rest and a day full of services and pastoral work of every sort, he returned ready for work at home on Monday morning.

"Mr. Collins rode to another church, equally distant, but he had a good road most of the way. I saw him come home in the evening, very tired, but Monday morning, bright and early, he is at work in the press.

"Mr. Waite spent the Sabbath at Nawng Fan, a Christian village, six miles distant, where a former head priest, a man influential and widely known, has recently become a Christian. Dr. McGilvary recently made a trip into the country of which he said: 'I wish I could photograph for you my last Me Pu Kah trip. The road was the worst I ever traveled. I rode back and forth in one ditch, almost swimming at times, in despair of finding a place where my horse would climb the bank. Finally after a super-equine effort my horse paused in equilibrium uncertain whether he would gain the bank, or tumble back in the mud. You can imagine my relief when the good horse really did scale the bank.' How is that for a boy of seventy-eight summers?

"But last Sabbath Dr. McGilvary spent the day teaching in the temple. Dr. McGilvary has spent more time in presenting the gospel to the priests than any other missionary. Many a man, now a Christian, got his first knowledge of the truth from him in a heathen temple."

While Dr. McKean is not an ordained minister, and medical work often detains him in the city, he shares most acceptably in the work of preaching the gospel. On the Sabbath in question, he preached in the city church in the morning, and at Ban Den chapel in the afternoon. The evening was given to a magic lantern service in the hospital chapel.

Gathering in the Harvest

The close of the year in Laos churches is October 31. In September and October, visits must be made to as many of the out-stations as possible, to examine classes of catechumens who have been under instruction during the year. The writer had an unusual number of out-stations under his charge in 1906, and so an unusual amount of paddling through Laos mud fell to his share that fall. A brief sketch of two of those trips must close the chapter.

Paddling Through Laos Mud

Horses were ready when school closed on Friday afternoon, and with Nan Chak, my cook and right-hand man, I rode southward from Lampoon along a fair road for six miles. Then the ponies had to swim two hundred yards in swollen waters, where, in the dry season, one may almost jump across. My faithful "Red Horse" already had a cough, and this trip was the last he was able to carry me. Reaching the other side, we again found a fair road most of the way to our first stop. Our carriers were already there, and the evening was spent in teaching the people to sing, and in instructing a catechumen class. One of its members, a young mother who had married an "outsider," had stood firm when he threatened to leave her if she did not give up the Christian religion. I felt that her faith had been tested, and was glad to receive her. The next morning horses had to be left behind. A boat ferried us across the "Big River," and with only Chinese trousers, a loose shirt and a hat, the writer was ready for wading. At the largest stream we expected to find a boat, but none was to be seen. The swift current made it hard to cross, but on the other bank at a native house we changed to dry clothing, and were none the worse. A visit to a backslider who was glad to see us but not yet ready to return, and a call at a non-Christian home where medical skill opened the way, occupied the time till we were ready to start. After floundering across four miles of rice plain, we spent Saturday night at the house of a teacher in the Chieng Mai girl's school. Three of her brothers, though attendants at Christian services, were not members of the church. All seemed impressed and asked to be received as catechumens. It was four miles farther to the chapel, and the Sabbath was without special incident further than that on the return in the afternoon the missionary managed to fall off the bamboo pole that constituted a bridge, into a little stream. The return on Monday morning was by the same route and uneventful.

Water Overhead On the other trip two weeks later, the horses could not carry us so far. Rain overhead was added to water under foot, and made the path so slippery that first one then the other carrier slipped down, but all was taken good-naturedly and no one was hurt. Six out of ten catechumens passed a creditable examination at that out-station and were gladly received. Arrangements were made to open a school. We returned Monday morning, wet to the skin, but happy in having found real progress where we had hardly expected it.

Touring by the Ladies of the Mission The position of woman among the Laos is so entirely free that there is not the same necessity for separate work on their behalf as in some fields. Nevertheless, many of the single, and some of the married ladies do some independent touring. Miss Fleeson in Lakawn and Nan spent considerable time in outside touring. In Dr. Campbell's absence on long tours, Mrs. Campbell has more than once visited the out-stations alone or with her children, and Mrs. Crooks, in Chieng Rai, has twice visited the Musu, a hill tribe, among whom we have Christians, when Dr. Crooks could not accompany her. Each vacation in the girls' school Miss Gilson makes it a point to visit the homes of her boarding pupils. On one of these tours she conducted a class for men at Muang Pao, sixty-five miles north of Chieng Mai, and brought back with her eight new pupils for the school. During the touring season, nearly every year one of the ladies of the mission has conducted regular classes for the women in some five different villages each week, thus riding a sort of circuit. Touring in Laos is more difficult for the ladies than for the men, and when ladies and children are of the party, the cavalcade is often a most picturesque one, for all that is needed to eat and wear, as well as tents, camp furniture and cooking utensils, must be carried.

CHAPTER XII

HOSPITALS AND HEALING AND HOW THEY HAVE HELPED

Missionary Medicine and Surgery

From the very beginning of work among the Laos, medical missions have helped to open the way for the gospel. Dr. McGilvary, the founder of the mission, and every missionary since, whether nominally a medical missionary or not, has been compelled to do medical work. Three scourges cause more suffering and death in "The Land of the Free" than all others combined—they are malaria, smallpox and vesical calculus, or stone. The last is perhaps more common than in any other part of the world, and only the surgeon can bring relief from its terrible pain. Surgery was entirely unknown among the Laos, as in most other parts of Asia, until the coming of the medical missionary. To-day, in the Chieng Mai and Lakawn hospitals, the surgeons in charge of each operate on some forty cases or more each year, in most instances successfully. The people have learned to trust the skill and loving care of the foreign physician. Had medical missions done nothing else than exemplify the love of Christ in the relief of such suffering, time and means would have been richly rewarded.

Malaria and Smallpox

In the early days of his work in Chieng Mai, Dr. McGilvary hired men to take the "white medicine," the name by which quinine has ever since been known there. Now it is sold in the market stalls of every city and many a village in the Siamese Laos states. Dr. McGilvary also introduced vaccination among them.

If anyone doubts the efficacy of vaccination, let him compare conditions forty years ago and to-day. Then parents expected that every child would have smallpox, and fully one third of them died of the scourge. To-day, throughout the great Chieng Mai-Lampoon plains, one seldom sees a case of smallpox. Why is this? Thirty thousand children have been successfully vaccinated during the past five years in that plain, by men sent out from our hospitals.

Opening Doors

Years have been added to the average duration of human life, and untold suffering subtracted. Instances need not be multiplied to make it plain that more than any other human agency, medical missions have prepared the way for the gospel among the Laos. Every week, every day in the year, in every mission station, the relief of human suffering is quietly exemplifying the gospel, disarming prejudice, opening doors, winning a hearing for the message of a Saviour's love. If you would win men to Christ, you must convince them, not only that the Saviour loves them, but that you love them and are ready to help them. In doing this, medical missions are a powerful, indirect evangelizing agency.

Direct Evangelism. Medical missions are also most fruitful as a direct evangelizing agency. Elder Pun, whom the writer left in charge of his work when he came to this country on furlough, was known twenty years ago as "Crazy Pun." Native physicians could do nothing for him, and friends finally took him to the dispensary in Chieng Mai, probably with little farther expectation than that, temporarily at least, they might be relieved of a burden. The missionary physician undertook the case. Gradually Pun's attacks of insanity became less frequent and less violent. He was allowed to return home, coming occasionally to the dispensary for treatment. The result was a complete cure. But while body and mind were being healed, he learned also of the Healer of souls. As he was taught to read with the use of the Bible, his mind and heart gradually opened to the truths. On his return home, in a quiet way he began to teach others and lead them as he had been led. Did he need a man to help him on the farm? Before the rice crop was harvested, he had taught him to read and led him to Christ. If he went on a journey, his heart was so full, he could but tell his fellow-travelers the good news he had learned. "Crazy Pun" had become Elder Pun, one of the wisest and most tactful of our evangelists. It must not be supposed, however, that he was employed at once, or soon, as a paid evangelist. It was because,

HELPERS, CHIENG MAI DISPENSARY

whether at home or abroad, in season and out of season, he was leading men and women to Christ, that the native church employs him as an evangelist at a wage hardly half of what he could earn in other ways.

A Group of Medical Assistants

All the assistants in the Laos hospitals and dispensaries are Christians. A group picture of four of those employed in the Chieng Mai hospital shows the kind of men with whom we work. Ai Lai, on the left, is in charge of the vaccine laboratory; Doctor Chanta, a Christian elder who for more than twenty years has given faithful service, and is now Dr. McKean's right-hand man in medicine and surgery, stands next; in front of him is Doctor Keo, hospital steward and head nurse, and at the right is Muang Chai, the second assistant, a younger man who is rapidly gaining in knowledge and skill.

No better example of a true medical missionary can be found than Doctor Keo, whose story Dr. McKean tells in these words:

"Sixteen years ago two men who had come three days' journey, appeared on our veranda. They were forlorn specimens of humanity, brothers, and both very ill. I shall never forget the confident manner with which they placed themselves and their ragged belongings at our door, seeming to say: 'Here we are at last. The missionary is our friend, we shall surely find relief.' Both were cured, and surely God sent them to us. One went back to his family and lived and died a Christian. The other, whose name is Ai Keo, remained in the hospital, became my assistant, and is now my steward and head nurse. His whole life and thought seem given to the service of God. Faithful to every duty, constant, kind and unselfish in his care of the poor sufferers who come to us, I verily believe Ai Keo has done more to comfort and relieve the sufferings of his own people than any Laos man who ever lived."

Although burdened with other duties, Ai Keo constantly teaches by word of mouth the truth his life exemplifies. For him, more completely than any other Laos man the writer knows, "to live is Christ."

A few years ago, Mr. Gillies was touring in the northern part of the province of Lakawn, in a district no missionary had ever visited before. He began to talk with a man from the village while he was waiting for his carriers. Very naturally, the villager asked his business. When Mr. Gillies told him he had come to tell of the "Jesus religion," the man immediately answered that there was a "Jesus man" in that village. Mr. Gillies soon found him and discovered that, several years before, this man had, for a short time, received treatment in the Lakawn hospital. He was unable to read, but had listened with earnest attention to the gospel in song and story as he heard it there. When the time came for him to leave, the missionary physician had bidden him remember what he had heard and come again soon. He was far from the city and had never returned, nor had an elder or other Christian ever visited him. But all alone, unable to read, with very little knowledge of the way, he had nevertheless torn down the spirit shrines and other signs of superstition, and had taught others as he had opportunity, what he had learned. He was known and respected in all the village as "the Jesus man." It was a pleasure to Mr. Gillies to remain some days in that village and deepen the impression this faithful disciple had already made, as well as further instruct and baptize the man himself.

Many other incidents might be told to illustrate the fact that medical missions, as a direct evangelizing agency, as well as indirect, are telling powerfully for Christ; but we must hasten on.

The Spirit Doctor

One of the greatest dangers that confronts our work is the liability of those who have already professed themselves Christians to be tempted back into heathenism when disease attacks them. It is a common belief of the Laos people that most diseases are the work of evil spirits, and the native doctor often refuses to prescribe until the customary offering has been made to the spirits. In his lonely village, far from the help of the missionary, the only believer in that village perhaps, what can the poor Christian do when sickness comes, when the life of his wife or child is at stake? What would you do?

The Trial of Faith.

When a man so situated says, as I have heard them say, "Living or dying, I am Christ's," it means more, requires a greater strength of faith to keep the resolution, than you or I can realize. Unless we can bring some knowledge of foreign medicine within their reach, we can hardly hope to hold true to their convictions the weaker members of our churches, when such emergency arises. The mission is trying to do just that.

Christian Native Physicians

In 1905 the dispensary in Chieng Mai sent out one hundred and fifty Christian vaccinators. These men were required to spend four days each month at the dispensary, where they received careful instruction, not merely in the art of vaccination, but in the use of common remedies for common diseases, and in the use of their Bibles. The small fee the government allows them to demand makes of them a body of self-supporting evangelists who reach many villages and districts which the foreign missionary has never reached, and their scalpel and little cases of medicine give them access to homes where even they would not be welcome as evangelists.

Self-Supporting Evangelists

Some of these men who have been sent out year after year, not only earn for themselves a fair living, but are becoming quite skillful in the treatment of ordinary diseases. They are becoming real medical missionaries to their own people. In His name they heal the sick, in his name they cast out demons, and in his name they preach the gospel of the kingdom. They not only bring the gospel to those who have never heard, but are able to hold true to their course many who are tempted in sickness to offer to the demons the sacrifices they and their fathers have been wont to offer, and so deny Christ. Medical work among the Laos people is not merely an evangelizing agency direct and indirect, but it is God's own means of conserving that which has already been won.

Equipment What equipment has the church in America provided for carrying on this important work? As one hears of the utterly inadequate buildings and instruments at the command of medical missionaries in some of the mission fields, one feels that the Philadelphia journalist who spent more than a year in visiting the mission fields of the world was in a measure justified, when, in view of such a niggardly policy he exclaimed to the men of the church, "Do the job or chuck it."

The Laos mission has received most generous treatment at the hands of the church. It only asks a continuance of the substantial interest shown in the past as new necessities arise. Moreover, the confidence and interest of both rulers and people in its medical work is shown in the fact that the whole current expense of all our dispensaries and hospitals is met by current receipts. Even for the enlargement of our older hospitals, they have come to depend on the generosity of those who have been benefited by their work.

More physicians and better equipment in the smaller stations are needed.

Chieng Mai Hospital

The means for the original buildings of Chieng Mai Hospital and Dispensary came from America, solicited by Dr. Marion A. Cheek, who gave fifteen years of faithful service to the work there. In recent years the hospital has been much enlarged through gifts from the native, the Chinese and the European merchants resident in Chieng Mai, and by the use of net current receipts. To-day it holds real estate and equipment worth at least twenty-five thousand dollars, and has comfortable accommodations for at least fifty patients, and residences for two physicians. Besides its native, its "princes'" and its foreign wards, its commodious chapel as well as its physicians' residences, it has a vaccine laboratory from which all the stations, and the government as well, draw their supplies of vaccine. Its most pressing need to-day is an adequate and modern operating room. No one who has not seen it can realize the extent and importance of the work that is being done there from day to day. If only because the whole mission looks to Chieng Mai as the seat of its projected medical school, it ought not to be obliged to wait for this much needed operating room where a group of students can conveniently see and assist, and where unsanitary conditions shall not endanger the results of the surgeon's skill. The illustration shows only the main building.

Chieng Mai Hospital, Northern Siam

Lakawn Hospital and Dispensary

In Lakawn the Van Santvoort Hospital and Dispensary are doing an in-patient work only a little smaller than in Chieng Mai. Its wards are of more recent construction and in some ways more convenient than those in Chieng Mai, and it has a better operating room. Its wards are often crowded, but the out-patient work and the sales of medicine are naturally smaller than in the great city and province of Chieng Mai. In recent years, the direct results of its work in men and women won to Christ have been a marked feature of work in Lakawn. We sincerely regret that circumstances make it doubtful whether Dr. Hansen will return to the work he has carried on so effectively.

Other Hospitals

A generous gift of ten thousand dollars as a memorial to a gentleman of Philadelphia has made possible the construction of an adequate hospital on modern lines in Chieng Rai, and the near future will see that important center for medical mission work well equipped, and exerting an influence that will be felt, not on Siamese soil alone, but far across the borders in British, and French Laos, and even up into China itself, for it stands on important caravan routes. A smaller building in Nan, erected mainly by use of the money paid the physician there by the Siamese Government for the care of the soldiers, gendarmes and civil officials stationed in that province, suffices for immediate needs. But in Pre there is no hospital, and only a dispensary building. Temporarily Pre has been without a missionary resident. If it is occupied again, and it must be, a hospital of adequate size should be built at once, and the growth of the work will soon demand larger hospital accommodation in Nan and in Lakawn.

The Favor of the Government

The King of Siam and his advisers have always taken an intelligent interest in the work of the American missions. But they have repeatedly shown an especial interest in the medical work. Many years ago, the Siamese Government gave to the missionary physician in Chieng Mai exclusive control of vaccination in the north. They have readily granted the use of land for medical mission purposes, and contributed both by moral influence and financial aid to success. Both the king and his brother, Prince Damrong, Minister of the Interior, as well as the crown prince and other high officials have repeatedly spoken in the highest terms of the medical work and treated with marked honor those engaged in it.

Work for the Lepers

No account of that work would be complete that did not tell of the work that has been planned and with the hearty approval of the government actually begun in Chieng Mai for the lepers of Siam. The grant by the Prince of Chieng Mai, confirmed by royal authority, of an island in the river near that city, has made a small beginning possible, but until the means for suitable buildings are in hand, only a small number of these sufferers can be provided for. No picture is likely to give to one who has never seen them an exaggerated idea of the poverty and misery of these poor outcasts. Dr. McKean, who has for many years interested himself in them, says in part:

"From time immemorial, leprosy has been known and feared in the Land of the White Elephant. Wandering about the streets and into the temples, or wearily hobbling through the bazaar in quest of alms, an offense to all beholders, a menace to the public, the leper is always and everywhere an object of profound commiseration. Very early in the disease, owing to stiffening and contraction of the muscles, loss of toes and fingers, and other deformities, the leper is wholly incapacitated from earning a living. His only means of subsistence is begging, his food scanty and coarse, his clothing mere rags. In the cold season, it is probable that not one of these sufferers passes a warm or comfortable night. If he does not sleep in the open where night overtakes him, his hut is at best unspeakably poor and mean. Buddhism does nothing for the leper; the government does nothing to relieve his distress. There is no hope for the betterment of his lot save from us who enjoy the blessings of a Christian civilization. Leprosy is incurable, but much can be done to ameliorate the condition of the leper. He is homeless, hungry, all but naked. In an asylum, shelter and warmth, food and clothing, will bring comfort to body and mind."

Such practical illustration of the spirit of Christ will open the lepers' hearts to the message that brings peace to the soul. This will assuredly prevent the spread of the disease. Hundreds of homeless lepers in our immediate vicinity know of our efforts in their behalf, and only await our invitation to come. We are even now caring for thirteen lepers in temporary huts of bamboo and thatch, but they and we are dependent upon the gifts of our friends in this favored land. Two thousand dollars will build a brick cottage and give a home to twenty leper men or twenty leper women. Twenty-five dollars will provide the entire support of an adult leper for one year. Twenty dollars will support an untainted child for a year. "Inasmuch as ye did it unto one of these my brethren, even these least, ye did it unto me."

CHAPTER XIII

SCHOOLS, THE PRESS AND CHRISTIAN LITERATURE

Constituency of the Schools

In the Laos field, as has already been said, school work followed rather than preceded evangelistic effort. No considerable number of "outsiders" have ever been enrolled in the schools. Some pupils have always come from non-Christian homes, but latterly, at least, the task of educating the children of Christians has been so large that little time or strength could be given to draw in others. The most notable exception is in the boys' school in Lakawn. There, quite a company of young priests who came to learn arithmetic and English, and held off from the religious exercises of the school, first listened, then began to share in the singing and Scripture reading. In addition, not a few boys and girls from the homes of Siamese and Laos officials have been enrolled as day pupils, rarely as boarders. Our schools give the best education to be had in the Laos states, and instruction in English and higher branches increasingly attracts intelligent and ambitious pupils. We hope ultimately to draw them to Christ as well as into our schools.

School Problems However, the problems of school work in the Laos mission are fundamentally two: To teach every Christian Laos boy and girl to read the Scriptures in his own language, and to educate the future leaders both of the church and of the community. Intelligent mothers, educated Christian men and officials are needed as well as evangelists and teachers. We need especially Christian physicians. Still, to raise up a native ministry, educated in our schools, is the problem that specially confronts the mission. "Young men for action, old men for council," so dominates the thought of the people, that so far our native ministers and evangelists are mostly men instructed in the Scriptures in adult years, and sent out to teach. As in the days of our Saviour in Judæa, the people would not readily listen to one under thirty years of age who taught publicly. As teachers in the schools, they welcome our educated young men and women, but the problem of a native ministry is as yet unsolved in the Laos field.

Village Schools. "A Christian primary school within the reach of every Christian Laos boy or girl," has been the watchword of the mission within recent years. Until ten years ago, little effort was made to establish village schools. The boarding schools in each station did primary work, but as the number of Christians and their desire for education increased, some change was necessary. The school accommodation, the time and the means given to primary work, were needed for pupils of higher grade. Little by little, though not yet entirely, the responsibility for this work has been laid on the members and elders of our churches. Self-supporting primary schools, attended sometimes by "outsiders," as well as Christians, have been gradually developed. Naturally the most conspicuous success has been attained where there is a considerable and prosperous native Christian community. Still, there as here, the teacher makes the school, and successful schools have grown up where outward conditions did not seem favorable. On the other hand, outstations which should maintain a good school often fail to do so. Still, each year sees a gain in the number and efficiency of self-supporting village schools. At its last report, the mission had twenty-two of them with over four hundred pupils.

Temple and Government Schools

Under the old régime, there was no provision for educating the women, but nearly one half of the boys spent a longer or shorter time in the Buddhist monasteries or temples, where they were taught to read and write, but learned little else. Since the Siamese Government tightened its hold upon the Laos provinces it has instituted many reforms and improvements. Conspicuous among them are the government free schools. Naturally these schools are conducted in the

Siamese language, but inasmuch as a good knowledge of Siamese is at present almost a passport to government employ, these schools are well filled, and as a whole do good work. They are still few in number, but a Siamese superintendent of education for the north is rapidly developing their number and efficiency.

Their Relation to Mission Schools

Education in the temples, being for boys alone and conspicuously inferior to that offered in the mission schools, the more that attendance there is impossible for a Christian, put no difficulty in the way of maintaining Christian village and boarding schools. Not so with the government free schools. They have developed a demand for Siamese that makes it necessary for mission schools, even in the villages, to teach Siamese.

As yet, no mission school has made that language the sole basis of instruction, as the government schools are doing, but it may be necessary in the end. The instruction in government schools is free, and where they are established the maintenance of mission schools in which tuition is charged is made more difficult. As yet, we cannot teach the Siamese language as well as they, and the loyalty of the Laos people to their own language is tested when we apply to them for support for the Laos schools. Mission schools must maintain their existence by their efficiency. In the boarding schools instruction in English has proved a great attraction. There is general demand for it, and some government schools teach it, but very imperfectly.

The Future While these government schools are less distinctly Buddhist than the temple schools, the influence and instruction, as well as some of the books they use, are not such as we wish for our Christian boys, and the government as yet makes little provision for the education of girls. Christian schools must be maintained, and their efficiency increased. Even in the Siamese language they must come up to the government standard. If they do so, the government may aid Christian schools as they do in India on the basis of inspection and examination. That problems have grown more difficult, must only increase our determination to solve them successfully. We welcome the government free schools and would coöperate with them for the education of all the people.

Boarding Schools I have spoken of the government schools in connection with our village, rather than our higher schools, because the former are more directly in peril. For our boarding schools, the rivalry is wholesome. It makes self-support more difficult, but what good school in America, or elsewhere, is supported by tuition fees? American schools are endowed, and higher schools in Laos, as in other mission lands, must be endowed, or receive a more generous annual support from mission funds. Without this, they cannot provide the education circumstances demand.

Chieng Mai Schools

The boarding schools for boys and girls in Chieng Mai are the oldest and largest in the mission. It is the purpose of the mission to maintain in them a higher grade than in other station schools. Pupils who have reached a certain grade in other schools, are expected to come to Chieng Mai for higher work. From Lakawn, from Chieng Rai, and from Pre, pupils have already been enrolled. These schools have almost ceased to do primary work, and the grade and quality of work done is being steadily raised. The Christian character of the instruction and influence is shown by the numbers from all the schools that are received each year into our church. True, most of them come from Christian homes, but if the schools do little for "outsiders," they are holding our young people true to Christ, and training them for leadership.

Prince Royal' College

Some years ago, the Crown Prince of Siam visited Chieng Mai, and was invited to lay the corner stone of William Allen Butler Hall, the new home for the boys' school. His Royal Highness was asked to give the school a new name. This he graciously did, calling it "Prince Royal' College." It does not yet do college work, but it must do so if it is to meet the demands of the near future. Every year sees further steps in that direction. It now has two missionary instructors, Messrs. Harris and

THE GIRLS' SCHOOL, CHIENG MAI

Palmer, and an efficient corps of native teachers trained in its own halls. About one hundred and twenty-five regular pupils are enrolled, and including a special term of instruction for teachers, its sessions continue ten months in the year. The normal class is held during the vacation of the regular school, and draws in, as it is planned to do, the teachers from village schools, both men and women, and from the boarding schools in other provinces. The training classes for evangelists, ministers and elders, have not yet been as closely associated with the college as they might be, but plans for the future include this. The missionary physicians have taught classes in physiology and hygiene, and several of the graduates of the school are in training in the hospital. As definite medical instruction develops, it is intended to make it a part of the work of the college. While it does not claim to measure up to its name, its plans are broad, and look to the development of a Christian college that shall be to the Christian Laos community and nation all that those words imply.

The Girls' School

While the girls' school in Chieng Mai does not reach as high grade, especially in Siamese and in English, as the college, the grade and quality of work done have steadily improved under the efficient leadership of Miss Gilson. Industrial work, especially sewing and weaving, are a prominent feature of the school, and aid in the direction of self-support. Here, too, some pupils are enrolled from other stations. The number of boarding pupils is even larger than in the college, although the total of boarding and day pupils is not quite so large. Its last report gave one hundred and fifteen pupils of whom sixty-six were boarders. The burden is far too heavy ever to be well carried by one missionary teacher, and we rejoice at the action of the board that looks to an increase in its faculty.

Lakawn Girls' School. The girls' school in Lakawn is a monument to the faith and efficiency of Miss Kate N. Fleeson, who opened the school and during most of the time until her death in 1906 continued to conduct it. Lakawn is a smaller city and province than Chieng Mai, so that the means at her command were smaller, but the attendance and the grade of work done in her school placed it fully on a par with the larger school. Its present comfortable building, occupied a short time before her death, was erected with materials and funds Miss Fleeson herself solicited, largely in Lakawn itself.

Lakawn Boys' School The boys' school in Lakawn will soon occupy the Kenneth Mackenzie Memorial building, a convenient and adequate brick structure, which means much for its future. Lack of adequate accommodation, and still more of means for current expenses, have hampered this important school in the past. "Is it good policy," said Dr. Taylor, its principal, "to pay several thousand dollars to place a missionary on the field and support him until he acquires the language, and then refuse two to three hundred dollars a year to enable him to do efficient work in his school?" It is hoped that in the future this lack will be supplied.

Other Boarding Schools

In Nan the Siamese commissioner showed his appreciation of the work of mission schools by offering to place a missionary in charge of the government school, pay all expenses and give him entire freedom to teach Christian truth. Difficulties stood in the way of accepting this offer. A boys' school has been established, but buildings and equipment are sorely needed. The schools in Pre and in Chieng Rai have been little more than day schools, and have drawn little from the treasury of the mission, but in Chieng Rai at least there is immediate demand for a school more adequate to the needs of that large and growing Christian community, second only to Chieng Mai in numbers and importance.

Theological and Biblical Instruction

When a large number of evangelists were regularly employed by the mission, it was easy to secure regular attendance on the training classes. In 1895 reduced gifts at home made it absolutely necessary to cease to pay evangelists and the burden was laid upon the native church. Even some of the best instructed and most efficient men had to turn to other employment. Since then, although the number of men sent out by the native church has gradually increased, and some have been regularly employed by the mission, training classes with a regular defined course have not been reëstablished. No new men have been ordained to the ministry, and as I have already said, the problem of adequate training now presses upon the mission.

Training Classes

Training classes are held each year in Chieng Mai and in other stations, and in some of the larger out-stations of the mission. These classes and uniform Bible lessons for the Sunday school have promoted a general knowledge of the Bible and its truths among the people. All realize that instruction in the Bible, both in Sunday school and in training classes, should be more thorough and systematic; but such is the pressure of work upon our small forces that this need has not yet been met.

The Press and Its Work

In the chapter "The Coming of the Gospel," it was stated that in the beginning of the work the Siamese Bible and hymn book and other Christian literature were used in schools and in public worship. The two languages are kindred, and the Siamese is the language of the rulers of the land. The Laos is written in a different character, and no type to print it was in existence. Not until 1893 did the arrival of the press and a font of Laos type put a Laos Christian literature within reach. Since that time the work of the press in Chieng Mai has gradually grown. It is not only the only press in the world equipped to print the Laos character, but it also does much printing in Siamese, in English and occasionally in French. Over three million pages are printed each year. Rather less than half of this is printed for the Bible Society and the mission, the balance is printed for the government and for other outside parties, and has made the press in recent years a self-supporting part of our work.

Laos Christian Literature

Matthew, a Catechism, and Laos reading books were first printed. An arithmetic, a geography, a Life of Christ, Pilgrim's Progress and a part of the Old Testament history, were reprinted with little change from the Siamese in which they had been originally written. It soon appeared that these Siamo-Laos books did not meet the need. A real Laos literature was called for and is gradually being supplied. One fourth of the Bible has been translated into the Laos language, and each year sees some addition to it. A General History, Bible Stories, a Life of Christ for Schools, Letters of See Mo (written from America by a native Laos man), Chandra Lela, A Story of Indian Life,—these indicate the range of the Christian literature our press is providing.

Still, only the beginnings of a vernacular Christian literature have yet been made. A Laos monthly paper, which gives a summary of the world's news, contributed articles of various sorts and comments on the Sunday school lesson, has a considerable circulation.

The Hymnal Rev. Jonathan Wilson, D. D., one of the two founders of the mission, has not only shared in Bible translation, but he has given himself especially to the preparation of hymns. He has translated more than five hundred of our best English and American hymns, and composed some original hymns in the Laos tongue. The Laos people are very fond of singing. Many a Christian who has only a small part of the Bible, carries his hymnal wherever he goes. Even non-Christian people sometimes join in singing these beautiful hymns, and the gospel is singing its way to the hearts of the Laos people, and will continue to do so when Father Wilson, our sweet singer, has passed away. Such tunes as "Onward, Christian Soldiers," "The Son of God Goes Forth to War," "Luther's Hymn," "Austrian Hymn," and "Aurelia," are constantly and well sung, in our Laos churches.

Other text-books for our schools and for our evangelistic classes, and Christian books for general reading, and still more, the balance of the Bible in their own tongue, are needs that the Laos church and mission recognize, and seek to supply. But such work, if it is to be well done, must be done slowly. As a whole, even our Christian Laos people are not a reading or a book-buying people. The growth of the schools and literature, with their common demands on the press must grow together.

CHAPTER XIV

THE NATIVE CHURCH

The Aim of Mission Work

Dr. Lawrence well said that the aim of Christian missions is to establish "a vital native church," and to "train it from the first in the principles of self-reliance, self-control and self-propagation." No hard and fast rule can be laid down by which we can measure the success of mission work, but the number of members enrolled tells far less than the establishment of a church such as Dr. Lawrence describes. Has the work among the Laos people developed such a church? A brief statement of the work that church is doing, with vignettes of some of its leaders, is the best answer to this question.

Early Growth of the Laos Church

I have said in another place that in the ten years from 1884 to 1894, the enrollment of the Laos church grew from one hundred and fifty-two to eighteen hundred and forty-one, a more than tenfold increase in ten years. In the ten years that followed, although the absolute increase was nearly as large, relatively it was far smaller. Does this mean that effort was less earnest, or less successful than in earlier years? Not necessarily.

The Situation in 1894

The Laos church found itself in 1894 with a large number of believers who were little instructed in Christian truth. Up to that time, the way to employment as evangelists and helpers, paid by the mission, had been rather easy. Persecution had practically ceased, and some had come into all the churches with a stronger impression of the privileges than of the duties of believers. Providentially, we doubt not, the necessity arose for a retrenchment. Evangelists could no longer be freely employed. Instead, the duty of contributing to the support of work among them, that had hitherto been paid for mainly out of foreign funds, was laid upon the churches.

Result of the Change

This sudden change of attitude on the part of the mission, however necessary it may have been, was difficult to understand. It took time for the church to adjust itself to the situation. Most of its leaders loyally accepted the burden laid on them, and increasingly year by year this initiative in Christian work has been taken by the churches. The members of the Laos church had never been " rice Christians," yet they had leaned upon the missionaries before 1894, and expected more moral and financial help than the mission has since then been able to give. The action of the mission taken in December, 1895, which definitely discontinued the old system of employing evangelists, was the " stirring up of the eagle's nest." It marked the end of the first stage of missionary effort among the Laos people.

The Meaning of the the Change An elder who was recently called as a witness in court says: "The judge and those around him, when I asked to take oath according to the religion of the Christians, asked me why I had entered the religion of the foreigners. I answered that it was not the religion of the foreigners, but the religion of the one true God for all the world." Whatever it may have been before, when the responsibility for native evangelists was laid upon and assumed by the native church, that church could no longer be called the church or the religion of the foreigner. For a few years accessions to the churches were smaller. Some who had professed themselves Christians ceased to attend services. Two or three churches were more seriously affected than the rest, and even to-day report a smaller membership than in 1894. But these changes were mainly a consolidation, a gathering of strength for a new advance.

Growth Since 1894 After three or four years when progress seemed small and doubtful, accessions to the churches began again to increase, and that increase has gone on steadily for ten years. Proportionally, accessions have never reached the standard of the ingatherings of 1884 to 1893, but in actual numbers received, 1908 surpassed any year that had preceded it, three hundred and thirty-one having been received on confession. The church has grown more in intelligence than in numbers; it has developed leaders and self-reliance; it has grown in all that makes the church of God a power on the earth. It has grown in its conception of what it means to be a Christian and in the standard of Christian conduct it sets up. The Laos church has to-day an "esprit de corps," and a standing in the community very different from anything it possessed in the days of its most rapid growth.

Present Needs

The writer wishes not to be misunderstood. The Laos church has not yet attained its majority. There is still much that discourages. Were missionaries withdrawn, the native church, which numbers hardly one communicant in a thousand of the native community, would find it difficult to stand and grow. The people need the moral support and encouragement, the guidance and constant help of the missionary. They need still more such a revival of vital religion, such a heart experience of God and his truth, as has been experienced in Manchuria and in other parts of China and of India. They need, the missionaries need, the church at home needs, a new baptism of the Spirit.

Self-Support

While an adequately trained and ordained ministry is lacking in the Laos field, and services almost everywhere are conducted by the elders, so that the local expenses are small, it still is true and important that no money from America goes to the support of any Laos church. In most cases, too, the church pays a part of the salary of evangelists and shares in the oversight of their work. A larger sum is contributed by the churches for native evangelists than is sent from America. The work of all the dispensaries and of the press is self-supporting. Primary schools in nearly every case are on a self-supporting basis. Chapels and churches are usually built, repaired and maintained by the gifts of the native church.

Self-Propagation It has already been said that to-day, the primary work of evangelism, reaching and drawing to Christ those who are not yet believers, is done mainly by native Christians. Their work is often clinched and completed by the visit and influence of the missionary, but in this, as in many other respects, we rejoice to see that the native Christian increases, while the missionary decreases.

Laos Conventions Nothing more vividly illustrates the growing strength of the Laos churches than the Laos conventions. The strongest church in a district, or different churches in turn, invite the members of other churches to be their guests, and a two to five days' programme of addresses, practical discussions and Bible study is arranged. An increasing share each year is taken by our native brethren. In twenty-three out of thirty-two services at Chieng Rai, they were the leaders. Held at a season of the year when little work is done in the fields, embodying something of the light-hearted good-fellowship that marks native festivals, giving to isolated Christians an opportunity once in a year to realize the meaning of Christian fellowship, these gatherings have become a regular part of the programme of the year. "The whole meeting," says Dr. Wilson in Lakawn, "was a time of good things from God that refreshed and gladdened us all." "The gathering in Chieng Rai," says Dr. Crooks, "was well attended and richly blessed of God."

A Contrast A son of the martyrs said in Me Dawk Deng at the convention: "These gatherings are great; why, I can recall the time when I knew every Christian," and he proceeded to count on his fingers. "We met in a small house in Dr. McGilvary's yard, just a handful of us. Those who passed by would peep through the fence and say, 'Witches! Witches!' Now what a change. Christians come to this convention from all over the land."

Foreign Mission Work Not only are they planning and giving and laboring for the evangelization of the districts near at hand, but more than once the native church has definitely committed itself to the work beyond the borders of Siam and among a population that is largely aboriginal, and understands little of the Laos tongue. In addition, companies of Christian women led by Mrs. McKean in Chieng Mai, and more recently in other stations, meet each month to study the mission fields of the world. Their contributions are divided between evangelistic work near home and work for the blind in Canton, China.

The Leaders Sketches of Kroo Nan Ta, our first native minister, and of Dr. Keo in Chieng Mai Hospital have already been given. I will close the chapter with vignettes of a pastor, a teacher, an evangelist, and a Christian business man, four Christian leaders from as many different provinces.

A Pastor—Kham Ai As an example of a pastor, I choose Kham Ai of Chieng Kham. Though never ordained, save as the first elder of the church in Nan, he was sent by that church to begin work in what is now its most important out-station. Whatever that growing group of believers is, it owes under God to this native pastor. A son of Christian parents in Chieng Mai, he had become a helper in the dispensary in Nan. His knowledge of medicine has been a constant help to him in his work. Nine days distant from Nan over high mountains, at best the missionary can visit him only once a year. His isolation and the dependence of the work on his individual effort is as complete as if he were a missionary in a foreign land, although this distant outpost is counted an integral part of Nan church.

A Teacher—Elder La In 1897, a boy of a good Christian family had nearly completed the course in the boys' school in Chieng Mai. He went to Chieng Mai soon after that station was opened, being employed in some capacity by one of the missionaries, and he married there. He already had shown himself apt to teach, and when a parochial, self-supporting school was begun in Chieng Mai, in 1898, he was its teacher. He gave excellent satisfaction, and became Sunday school superintendent and elder, as well as village teacher. That school has grown in numbers and in importance with the growth of the Christian community, and now has four teachers of whom he is the leader. Less highly trained than some other teachers in the mission, he still is, so far as the writer is aware, the senior of them all in continuous, faithful service. Personally, the writer looks to him and men like him, trained in our boarding schools, then employed as teachers, to supply the need of a trained ministry.

An Evangelist—Nan Pun

Nan Pun had been employed at a good salary as an "assistant" to the English engineer in charge of railway surveys. In 1905 he met with a serious injury which will make him lame for life, and was sent to the mission hospital in Lakawn. He was already an educated and exceptionally intelligent man, as his title Nan shows, and the study of the Scriptures convinced him that only in Christ, not in Buddha, could he find rest and salvation. When he recovered he at once asked to be baptized. Although a lucrative government position was offered him, he gladly remained as teacher in the boys' school at less than half the salary, that he might study to be an evangelist. His first concern was for his family in Lampoon. So far only one of them has yielded to his persuasions, but with his wife's relatives in Pre, he has been more successful. Six homes in their village have torn down the spirit shrines and declared themselves Christians. Still, during term time, Nan Pun is a teacher and student. In the vacations, he is active as an evangelist, even if he is lame. He is one of the most promising of all our helpers, and despite his youth, a leader in Lakawn.

A Christian Business Man—See Mo

About 1885 a returning missionary from Laos brought with him to America the son of Nan Chai, one of the earliest Christians in Chieng Mai, and a man of considerable means. Though See Mo came no farther than San Francisco and remained there only a year, he is the only Laos man who has seen as much as that of the "outside country." His letters descriptive of what he saw in strange lands have been printed by the press, and are much read by his countrymen. He is an elder in Chieng Mai church, a merchant and a timber dealer, perhaps the man of largest means in the native church. He occupies a most comfortable house, built after the foreign style, though adapted to native use. He is a reader of several American and English periodicals, speaks English perfectly and is an earnest Bible student and superintendent of the Sunday school. He was appointed chairman of a commitee of the native presbytery to foster and support Christian village schools. He is but one of a dozen Christian business men who might be named, mostly men educated in our schools, busy men but ever ready to give time and thought to the interests of the coming kingdom.

CHAPTER XV

OPPORTUNITIES, OUTLOOK, NEEDS

An Open Door

The question is often asked, why have the Laos people proved more open to the gospel than others on whom Buddhism has laid its hand? The answer seems to be somewhat as follows:

First. Scratch the Laos Buddhist, and you find a spirit-worshiper, Spirit worship, not Buddhism, was the original, is the actual, religion of the Laos people. Their sense of spiritual realities makes it easier to present to them a spiritual religion.

Second. Another fact closely related to this, is that the Laos are a more religious people than the Siamese or the Burmese. This is probably because the deadening, atheistic tendencies of Buddhism have had less influence upon them.

Third. To men and women who, from their earliest recollection, have lived in fear of the demons, the gospel of a loving Saviour who can and will drive out the evil spirit, comes with a message of deliverance. Once understood, it appeals to them in a way that we in Christian America hardly understand.

Fourth. The Messianic hope of Buddhism, scarcely known in Burma, less emphasized among the Siamese, gives to the gospel a point of approach to the heart of every thoughtful Laos man or woman. "He for whose coming you long has already come."

Fifth. The comparatively high moral standards of the Laos, not derived from Buddhism, but a part of their national inheritance and character, have prepared the way for the coming of the gospel.

Circumstances That Have Helped

Had the missionaries gone to the Laos in 1835, when Dr. Bradley began work among the Siamese, they would have found political conditions so confused, and life and property so insecure, that perhaps little could have been accomplished. British rule in Burma, and more direct enforcement of Siamese authority in the Laos states, have prompted peace, protected the persons of the missionaries, and given time and opportunity to the people to listen to their message. Changing political and social conditions, an awakened interest in education, increasing knowledge of the world, or desire for such knowledge, make the leaders of the people to-day peculiarly open to new influences, religious as well as social.

Methods That Have Helped

The emphasis placed at the first upon evangelistic effort has never ceased to be a marked feature of mission work among the Laos. Whatever institutional or routine work may fall to their share, all missionaries—the women as well as the men—are expected to share in hand-to-hand evangelistic work. Of this work schools have been the result, not the precursors. The school has not been needed to open the way into the home, but rather to train the children of homes already open. Medical work is useful in all fields, but more perhaps than in most fields medical work has among the Laos won friendship, removed prejudice and opposition, and exemplified the real meaning of the gospel.

Difficulties to Be Met

That indifference to all spiritual facts and realities which is a marked result of Buddhist teaching, is the greatest obstacle mission work must overcome. Neither the Laos nor any other non-Christian people can be said to be hungering for the gospel. Individuals may show themselves prepared for its reception, but only a Christian heart full of love and helpfulness can overcome indifference and awaken desire for higher things.

A second obstacle is the ties of kindred, of friendship and of custom. To convince a Laos man or woman of the truth is easier than to persuade him to break away from these ties and follow Christ. Of open persecution there is now little; of secret opposition, of the inertia that is slow to break with the past or allow others to do so, there is still much. The warp of Buddhism and the woof of spirit worship are so interwoven in the whole life of the people that it requires much faith and courage to break away.

Finally, although moral conditions are vastly better than in India or China, even when indifference is overcome, when despite opposition, decision for Christ has been made, we must still constantly remember in dealing with the new convert the pit out of which he was digged. Offenses against the moral law among professed Christians often sadden the missionary. He must often remember the injunction, "Ye who are spiritual, restore such a one in a spirit of gentleness."

The Outlook

First. We are encouraged by the growing self-dependence of the native church. Its leaders welcome the missionary as counselor, friend and teacher, yet often reverse the situation and really become themselves his advisers and leaders. God grant that this may increasingly be true as the years go on!

Second. The number in the Laos land who incline to accept the truth, but have not yet broken away from old ties, as well as of earnest inquirers, is increasing. We pray and labor for, and we must expect in the near future, a larger turning to God than we have yet seen. May we be ready in the day of his power!

Third. The very fact just stated, and the open door among the native leaders, emphasize the danger lest, if we do not enter with the gospel, these doors may be closed. Commercialism, absorption in material things, the rush of modern life, all are coming in like a flood. Even to-day many of the young men, particularly those who are under the influence of Siamese officials, are less open to the gospel than they were five years ago. Less universally perhaps than in China and Korea, but nevertheless truly, it is a time of crisis in Laos.

Fourth. It must be kept in mind that promising as conditions are in some parts of the land, the great bulk of the area and of the Laos people are still totally untouched by the gospel. French and Chinese Laos are among the great unoccupied fields of the world. Even in Siam itself, half the Laos people are entirely beyond the reach of our organized work, and of those within reach only a small proportion have really heard the gospel. Of the Laos in Siam, only one in one thousand is a member of our church. On the average, each Laos missionary finds an area as large as several counties and a population of two hundred thousand persons accounted his parish, with two hundred scattered, imperfectly instructed believers, most of them very poor in this world's goods, as his working force. I ask once more, in view of the vastness of the field yet to be reached, in view also of the burden of the work upon the mission and of the responsibility for that work that God lays upon the church at home:

Is the Presbyterian Church in the United States of America planning for anything less than the conquest of the whole Laos race for Christ?

What ought the church, what ought you, to do?

Needs

First. Larger income for educational work is counted by the mission its most pressing present need. The grade of our higher schools must be raised, and we should be able to accept all qualified pupils even if they cannot pay much tuition. We must train the leaders.

Second. The force of missionaries must be so increased that furloughs can be taken without crippling the work. Existing stations must be fairly manned. At present, even when all are on the field, not a single station can be said to be adequately manned.

Third. Foreign funds should be available for evangelistic work, so that we can assure our helpers of regular and continuous employment at wages not too much below the compensation in other employment. We should be able to say to a church: If you will send out one evangelist we will send another to travel and work with him. We expect the native church to do its share, but we must coöperate with and help them.

Fourth. We need missionaries and native helpers to go into the regions that are beyond the limits of our present stations, and organize and man new stations. Expenditures for houses, for dispensaries and for school buildings are to be provided.

Above all, the Laos church needs that, by a fuller knowledge of its needs, the church at home may be able to pray more intelligently for the work in the fair Land of the Free, and more heartily to coöperate with the Christians at work there. If the church at home does its share, with the blessing of Him in whose name we all labor, we may surely hope to see the Laos race brought to Christ in our day and generation. That he may live to see this is the hope and prayer of the writer of these lines.

QUESTIONS FOR STUDY

The following questions have been prepared for the use of those studying this book. In accordance with the Announcement facing Chapter I, which all leaders of classes should read with care, questions on Chapters V to IX have been omitted.

The purpose of these questions is not merely to review the text, but to promote independent thought and discussion. Review questions, appealing merely to memory, are of value only as preliminary to discussion and can easily be framed by any person of average intelligence. The questions given below demand the exercise of individual judgment as well as knowledge of the text; in a few cases the text will be found of no aid whatever.

It is not supposed that the average student will be able to answer all these questions satisfactorily or that all students will agree in their conclusions. It is intended rather that students shall come to the class session with questions unanswered and opinions sometimes in opposition, so that there may be a real basis for discussion.

Some of these questions may be specially indicated by the leader for discussion at the following session. In no case will it be advisable to try to cover the entire list. Better concentration on a few well-adapted questions than a hurried review of all. Circumstances will determine the selection for each class. For some the main value of the questions will be to suggest others that are better.

In working out the questions the free use of pencil and paper is recommended. Ideas which are the result of reflection should be jotted down, and pertinent passages in the text once more consulted for further light. The mere attempt to formulate usually helps to stir up new ideas that would not otherwise arise. All this tends to give an appetite for the class session.

Questions on Chapter I

1. How would you state the missionary responsibility of the Christian church?

2. How would you determine the missionary responsibility of any single Christian denomination?

3. To what extent is the responsibility of any church determined by the average of what other churches do?

4. What can you say as to the responsibility of the Presbyterian Church (North) at home?

5. What can you say as to its responsibility abroad?

6. Name all the points you can that give one field a greater claim than another.

7. How far should the quality of its people affect the claim of any field?

8. How far should the strategic position of a field as a base for future operations affect its claim?

9. How far does exclusive occupation of a field affect its claim on the occupying body?

10. For what missionary work in the world is the Presbyterian Church exclusively responsible?

11. How do the Laos compare in number, for example, with the North American Indians?

12. How do they compare in probable future influence?

13. How does their field compare with that of the North American Indians as a base for future operations?

14. How does it compare in the number of Christian agencies engaged?

15. Name the advantages to missionary work of having a single language for a large population, as is true for the Tai race.

16. What are the advantages for the missionary of approaching a new people with a previous knowledge of their language?

17. How will this widespread knowledge of a language affect the work of native evangelists?

18. How long do you think it would take you to become a really effective preacher in a new language?

19. How are the problems of missionary literature complicated by having several languages in a single field?

20. Why is a time of transition in any field especially important for missionary work?

21. How many missionaries would we have in the United States if it were manned no better than the Laos field? *

22. How many missionaries would you have in the state in which you reside?

23. Sum up the claim of the Laos field upon the Presbyterian Church.

* See Appendix B.

Questions on Chapter II

1. Why cannot the religions of Asia take any credit for the high position of woman among the Laos?

2. Which is better, the Chinese custom that a wife enter the husband's family, or the Laos custom that the husband enter the wife's?

3. What is the effect upon the wife in the former instance?

4. What is the effect upon the character of the husband in the latter instance?

5. Contrast with this the Christian custom that the young people set up a separate home.

6. What would be the practical effects of the Laos custom of inheritance?

7. Contrast divorce among the Laos with that among the Mohammedans.

8. What are the advantages and disadvantages of such strict observation of custom as obtain among the Laos?

Questions on Chapter III

1. What do you consider the strongest point in Buddhism as seen among the Laos?

2. What are its worst features?

3. Why do you think it succeeded in spreading as it has among the Laos?

4. Compare the Ten Commandments of Buddha with those of Moses, and state the main differences.

5. Give reasons why you approve or disapprove of the last five Commandments of Buddha.

6. Compare the Ten Commandments of Buddha with the two great Commandments given by Jesus Christ, and state the difference.

7. What do you think would be the practical effect on life of the doctrine of Karma?

8. What would be the practical effect upon life of ignoring the existence of God?

9. What would be the practical effect of the doctrine of merit?

10. What has Christianity to learn from Buddhism as to methods of approach?

11. What practical advantages has Christianity over Budhism in seeking to win the Laos?

12. How much effort do you think it is worth that the Laos should have Christianity instead of Buddhism?

Questions on Chapter IV

1. Have you ever known anyone who was superstitious in any way?

2. How do you account for such feelings?

3. Which is the best guard against superstition, Christianity or common sense?

4. Try to imagine the practical effect upon your own life of a belief in evil spirits.

5. What effect would it have upon your perseverance?

6. What effect would it have upon planning far in advance?

7. How would you show that Buddhism is not good enough for the Laos?

8. What are the practical evils of the belief in witchcraft?

9. What practical advantages has Christianity over spirit worship in seeking to win the Laos?

10. How much effort do you think it is worth that the Laos should have Christianity instead of spirit worship?

Questions on Chapter X

1. What responsibility has the Presbyterian Church assumed in occupying a field where no other Christian bodies are at work?

2. What do the results of Mr. Caswell's tutorship indicate as to the importance of work for ruling classes?

3. What sort of missionaries are needed for such work?

4. For what various reasons do you think Dr. McGilvary might be called a great missionary?

5. Why is it that new religions are so often persecuted?

6. What are the advantages and disadvantages of persecution to the church?

7. What would you infer as to the character of heathen religions from the fact that those away from home are so much easier to win?

8. Give several reasons why growth in a mission field should be more rapid after a couple of decades.

9. What are the relative advantages of missionaries and converted natives as evangelists?

10. Is the mission right in encouraging the Laos Christians to undertake work in French territory so far from home?

11. Formulate the responsibility of the Presbyterian Church for the Laos-speaking people of South China.

Questions on Chapter XI

1. Is the main duty of the missionary to preach the gospel?

2. What do you mean by preaching the gospel?

3. In what ways would the work of the evangelistic missionary differ from that of a preacher in America?

4. What are the main arguments for spending time in training natives to do evangelistic work rather than in direct preaching?

5. To what extent do you think these arguments hold good for church work in America?

6. Give the arguments for intensive as opposed to extensive work and vice versa.

7. What should be the main aims of a missionary in an occasional visit to a station?

8. Do you think that Christians in America would thrive under such occasional oversight?

9. Who is ultimately to blame that there are not more converts in these villages?

10. Which do you think are most in need of pastoral oversight, Laos Christians or Christians in America? why?

11. Study the table of distances and travel on page 125 and try to discover places in America that are as far removed from each other in point of time as are the Laos stations.

12. If you had to meet in your Christian work the same physical difficulties that the Laos missionaries meet in their touring, would you consider that you had a right to neglect it?

13. What in your opinion are the principal needs of evangelistic work among the Laos?

14. Whose business is it to see that these needs are met?

Questions on Chapter XII

1. What is the main purpose of medical missions?

2. Would medical missions be justified if there was no opportunity for direct evangelistic work in connection with them?

3. Are Christian people justified in maintaining hospitals in this country which make no attempt to evangelize their patients?

4. What are the special advantages of medical over other forms of missionary work?

5. What are its disadvantages as compared with other forms?

6. In what ways can a hospital be most effectively made a direct evangelistic agency?

7. What rules should a missionary follow in the employment of evangelists?

8. What evidence does the chapter present to you that the Laos do become genuine Christians?

9. If isolated Laos Christians relapse under temptation, where would you locate the final responsibility?

10. Do you think it is wise to send out as teachers of Christianity men who know so little as the vaccinators?

11. Why is it important to have well-equipped hospitals among the Laos?

12. How is this equipment to be secured in view of the lack of funds at the disposal of the board?

Questions on Chapter XIII

1. Name the purposes of missionary schools in such a field as the Laos in what you consider the order of their importance.

2. Indicate the sort of equipment that would be needed to carry out these purposes.

3. What advantages has educational over other forms of missionary work?

4. Should we be justified in spending time teaching non-Christians if no conversions resulted?

5. What is the justification of maintaining schools at all when government schools exist?

6. What course of studies should you recommend for the Laos as compared with that of schools in America?

7. State what appear to you to be the principal needs of Laos schools.

8. Why do you think the board sometimes pursues what seems like a poor business policy in equipping schools?

9. What are the special advantages of boarding schools on the mission field?

10. What sort of training do you think a prospective educational missionary should have?

11. Present the relative claim of America and Laos upon a Christian normal school graduate who is free to go.

12. Why is it important to compose and not merely to translate the vernacular literature?

13. How do you think the demand for literature could be stimulated among the Laos?

Questions on Chapter XIV

1. If the aim of missions is to found a self-supporting native church, when is the time to begin to teach self-support?

2. Does the experience of 1894 indicate any previous mistake on the part of the missionaries?

3. Because retrenchment proved a blessing does it follow that it would be better to cut down appropriations to all missions?

4. In what ways might retrenchment be a blessing to the work at home?

5. What needs can be provided by the church at home for the native church without fear of pauperizing it?

6. What things should the native church be expected to provide for itself?

7. If the native church cannot pay for these things, should mission funds be used for the purpose, or should it be obliged to go without?

8. What are the advantages and disadvantages of making the demands upon native Christians very light?

9. What are the advantages and disadvantages of having Christianity comparatively popular?

10. What responsibility is laid upon missionaries when Christianity is popular?

11. Should the chief emphasis then be laid upon extensive or intensive work?

12. How do these principles apply to the work of the home church?

13. Should Laos Christian conventions be made as like or as unlike the native festivals as possible?

14. Give several reasons why the Laos seem to you a people worth helping.

Questions on Chapter XV

1. What circumstances constitute for any field a special claim on the missionary activity of the church?

2. Which of these circumstances are present in the case of the Laos field?

3. Sketch the main points of the gospel message that you think would be most attractive to the average Laos.

4. In what way would you present the gospel in order to overcome indifference?

5. How do you think it would be best to deal with the difficulty of the ties of custom?

6. How would you recommend to deal with the breach of moral discipline in the native church?

7. How will the entrance of commercialism affect the spirit of independence and the old customs?

8. How will it affect morality and indifference towards the gospel?

9. Sum up the reason why the present is a time of special opportunity.

10. What would be the Christian force in your state if it were no better provided than the Laos field?

11. How many states adjoining your own would equal in population the over four million Laos in French and Chinese territory?

12. Is there any other field for which the Presbyterian Church alone is responsible that is so inadequately cared for?

13. Sum up the appeal which the Laos field makes to the Presbyterian Church.

APPENDIX A

PRONUNCIATION OF PROPER NAMES

ai, in Mai and Rai, as in *aisle*.
ao, in Pao and Dao, like *ow* in *cow* (Yankee dialect).
e in Me, as in *men*.
Chieng, almost like chung.
u in Muang, like German ü.
Pit-sa-nu-lok, accent on last syllable (lōke).
Sala, accent on last syllable, sa-lah′.

APPENDIX B

DISTRIBUTION AND WORK OF THE PRESENT FORCE OF THE LAOS MISSION

NOTE.—In brief compass it is not possible to tell all the work assigned to the various members of the mission. Besides, furloughs often make changes necessary, temporarily at least. The effort is to designate the characteristic work of each missionary when on the field. Accordingly, no mention is made either of furloughs or of temporary assignments.

The figures in parentheses, following the name, show the date of appointment.

CHIENG MAI

Rev. Daniel McGilvary, D. D. (1858), Mrs. McGilvary (1860). Evangelistic work, particularly in the temples, literary work.

Rev. and Mrs. D. G. Collins (1886). The Press. Charge of three out-stations.

James W. McKean, M. D., and Mrs. McKean (1889). In charge of the hospital and dispensary. Bible translation. Laos monthly. Two out-stations.

Howard Campbell, D. D., and Mrs. Campbell (1894). In charge of Chieng Mai church. Itineration. Bible translation. Mrs. Campbell has charge of the Phraner Memorial Primary School.

Rev. J. H. Freeman (1895), Mrs. Freeman (1892). Care of the churches and of the evangelistic and medical work in the Province of Lampoon. (Their residence is Lampoon city, seventeen miles from Chieng Mai.) Preparation of the Sunday school helps. Women's classes.

Rev. William Harris, Jr. (1895), Mrs. Harris (1889). Principal of Prince Royal College. Mission Treasurer. Charge of Me Dawk Deng Church.

Miss Edith M. Buck (1903). Teacher and Matron in Girls' School.

Miss Mabel Gilson (1904). Principal of Girls' School.

Rev. and Mrs. M. B. Palmer (1906). Vice Principal of the College. Charge of three out-stations. Together they train the schools and church in singing.

Claude W. Mason, M. D., and Mrs. Mason (1906). Medical work. Two out-stations.

LAKAWN (65 miles east and south of Chieng Mai)

Rev. Jonathan Wilson, D. D. (1858). Evangelistic work. Hymn translation.

Rev. Roderick Gillies (1902) and Mrs. Gillies (1891). Evangelistic touring. Charge of Boys' School.

Charles H. Crooks, M. D. and Mrs. Crooks (1904). Charge of Van Santvoort Hospital. Medical itineration. Literary work.

Rev. and Mrs. Howells Vincent (1903). Charge of church. Itineration. Direction of building new Boys' School.

Miss Elizabeth Carothers (1904). Charge of Girl's School. Women's classes.

Miss Eula VanVranken (1906). Teacher in Boys' School.

PRE (70 miles southeast of Lakawn)

Rev. and Mrs. C. R. Callender (1896). Church and evangelistic work.

Edwin C. Cort, M. D. Medical work. Language study.

NAN (90 miles northeast of Pre, 160 miles due east of Chieng Mai)

Rev. S. C. Peoples, M. D., D. D., and Mrs. Peoples (1882). Medical work and touring.

Rev. Hugh Taylor, D. D., and Mrs. Taylor (1888). Church and school work.

CHIENG RAI (125 miles northeast of Chieng Mai)

Rev. W. C. Dodd, D. D. (1886) and Mrs. Dodd (1887). Evangelistic touring. Charge of church and work in Keng Tung. Literary work.

Rev. W. A. Briggs, M. D. (1890))and Mrs. Briggs (1892). Medical and evangelistic work. Charge of local church.

Rev. and Mrs. Henry White (1902). Evangelistic work. School work. Charge of churches south of the city. Women's classes.

Rev. Lyle C. Beebe (1908). Language study. Charge of churches north of the city.

REINFORCEMENTS, 1909 (Station not yet assigned)

Rev. Wm. O. Yates. Language study. Touring.

Miss Lucy Starling. Language study. Teaching.

APPENDIX C

STATISTICS OF THE LAOS MISSION

Statistics given are in every case the latest available; for the missionary force, 1909; for the native church and work, 1908 except where no data later than 1907 are at hand.

Missionary Force

Ordained Men	17	
Doctors (two ordained)	6	21
Wives	17	
Single Ladies	5	22
Total Foreign Missionaries		43

Native Helpers (*Incomplete*)

Ordained Native Ministers	4
Native Evangelists	30
Teachers—Men, 30. Women, 12. Total	42
Bible Women	4
Medical Assistants	20
Press Employees	24
Vaccinators (Four months in year)	125

Native Contributions (*Incomplete*)

For Church Expenses	Rs	178.49
For Schools	"	210.21
For Missions	"	113.09
Total contributions	Rs	501.79
Equal	$	167.09

Church Statistics

Organized Churches (none aided)	18
Stations and Out-stations	74
Total Communicants	3,705
Additions on Confession During 1908	331
Sabbath School Pupils	2,923

School Statistics

Boarding Schools	5
Day Schools	24
Pupils, about	450
Attendance Training Classes, reported about	135
Total under instruction, about	585

Press Report

Pages printed:

For Bible Society and Mission	1,403,800
For outside parties	1,314,770
Total	2,718,570

INDEX